Flower Gardening in the Hot Midwest

Flower Gardening in the Hot Midwest

USDA ZONE 5 AND LOWER ZONE 4

Linda Hillegass

University of Illinois Press
Urbana and Chicago

The photos on pages ii, 14, 138, 170, and 182 are by James L. McKee.
Except where noted, all other photos are by Linda Hillegass.

Library of Congress Cataloging-in-Publication Data
Hillegass, L. L.
Flower gardening in the hot Midwest : USDA zone 5 and lower
zone 4 / Linda Hillegass.
p.   cm.
Includes bibliographical references (p.) and index.
ISBN 0-252-02576-8 (cloth : acid-free paper) —
ISBN 0-252-06885-8 (paper : acid-free paper)
1. Gardening—Middle West. I. Title.
SB453.2.M53.H56   2000
635.9'0977—dc21   99-050670

1 2 3 4 5 C P 5 4 3 2 1

To Jim McKee, the one and only

Contents

Acknowledgments

Thanks to the three gardeners who inspired me to write this book. Clayton Kurkowski called me "gardener extraordinaire" one day and it went to my head. Deb Evnen swelled my head further by asking a thousand gardening questions for which I realized I had answers. Finally, my mother, Catherine MacDonald, told me I should write a gardening book the way I write letters to my loved ones.

Further thanks to two friends who encouraged me to write the book in the first place, gave me invaluable comments when the manuscript was completed, and never flagged in their confidence in the book's worth: Penny Rickard and Kris Gilbertson of Capability's Books. Thanks, too, to Aileen Rodgers and Deb Evnen for reading the manuscript and making suggestions and to Karen Hewitt at the University of Illinois Press for believing in and shaping this book.

And special thanks to my husband, Jim McKee, who gave me a well-timed kick in the pants when writer's block threatened to swamp the whole project.

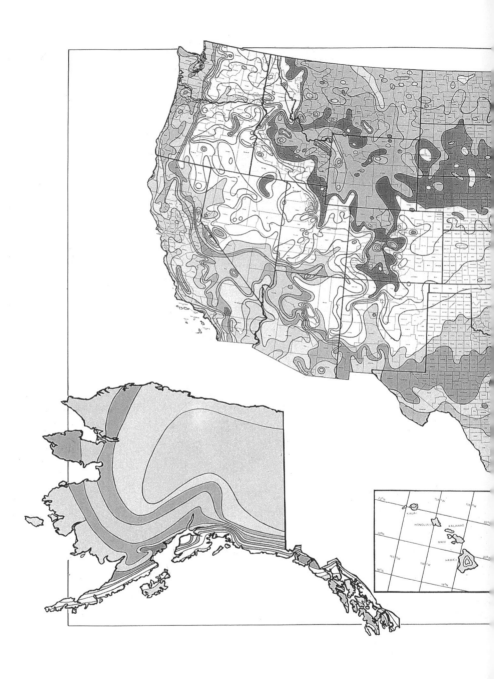

United States Department of Agriculture Plant Hardiness Zone Map (Agricultural Researc

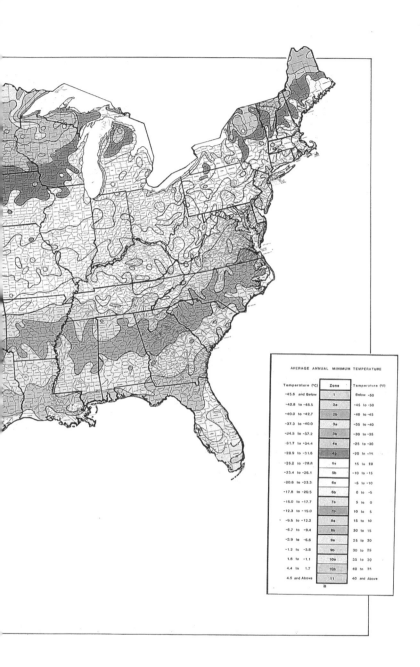

AVERAGE ANNUAL MINIMUM TEMPERATURE

Temperature (°C)	Zone	Temperature (°F)
-45.6 and Below	1	Below -50
-42.8 to -45.5	2a	-45 to -50
-40.0 to -42.7	2b	-40 to -45
-37.3 to -40.0	3a	-35 to -40
-34.5 to -37.2	3b	-30 to -35
-31.7 to -34.4	4a	-25 to -30
-28.9 to -31.6	4b	-20 to -15
-26.2 to -28.8	5a	15 to 20
-23.4 to -26.1	5b	-10 to -15
-20.6 to -23.3	6a	-5 to -10
-17.8 to -20.5	6b	0 to -5
-15.0 to -17.7	7a	5 to 0
-12.3 to -15.0	7b	10 to 5
-9.5 to -12.2	8a	15 to 10
-6.7 to -9.4	8b	20 to 15
-3.9 to -6.6	9a	25 to 20
-1.2 to -3.8	9b	30 to 25
1.6 to -1.1	10a	35 to 30
4.4 to 1.7	10b	40 to 35
4.5 and Above	11	40 and Above

ervice, USDA).

Flower Gardening in the Hot Midwest

1

Coping with the Climate

A garden is often described as a paradise, but if you live in the hot Midwest, the climate can make it seem more like hell. The farm belt that stretches across the heartland of America is great for corn, but raising flowers here can be a challenge. From central Nebraska east to Indiana lies the heart of USDA zones 4 and 5, a strip of blessedly rich soil and a hellish climate of extremes.

Winter temperatures in our area drop as low as −10 to −25 degrees Fahrenheit. Summer temperatures can zoom up over 100 degrees. It's true that many parts of the country experience high heat. Others routinely face icy winters. Only in the hot Midwest are we up against both winter temperatures well below zero and the prolonged scorching heat, drought, and unstoppable winds of summer.

Although parts of the northeastern United States share our USDA hardiness zones and can relate to the challenges of cold weather, our Midwestern summers make New England weather look like sissy stuff. New York sees only *seven to thirty days* a year when the temperature is above 86. By contrast, South Dakota, Nebraska, northern Kansas, southern Iowa, northern Missouri, Illinois, and southern Indiana can expect *thirty to sixty days* in that range.

Putting further demand on flowering plants is our area's propensity to shoot from one extreme of temperature to the other in just a few hours. Our landlocked midcontinental position means we are not subject to the moderating influence that large bodies of water exert on temperature. An unusually warm winter day may be followed by frigidity, the temperature plummeting sixty-five degrees from one day to the next. A summer thunderstorm can drop the temperature from 100 degrees to 60 degrees in a matter of minutes.

Snow is intermittent in a zone 5 winter, providing no reliable insulating cover. Rain on the farm belt is adequate in spring and fall but normally sparse in the blasting heat of summer. Winds are ever present and sometimes violent. The sun's rays are very strong and direct.

You can make your garden a paradise in spite of all this by choosing plants carefully and learning to cope with the climate. Reading about gardening is a great way to learn, but unfortunately most books on the subject are written by gardeners from England or the Pacific Northwest, where less extreme climates and the blessings of reliable rainfall create gardening environments wholly unlike ours. There is also a great outpouring of garden literature from New England. This has much to say about harsh winters, but does not address the heat and drought of summer. Garden books foreign to our region describe, too, a sequence of bloom that doesn't translate to the exceptionally long bloom season of the Midwest.

Heat Wave

Temperatures above 100 degrees do not occur every year, but when they do they can last several days. A flowering plant sited in full sun will experience great stress. Add the wind that can come right along with the heat and only the tough will survive. In a recent Nebraska heat wave, the wags at a local radio station fried eggs on the sidewalk. No wonder your flowers look cooked in this climate. Careful attention to USDA hardiness zones in selecting plants will see your garden reliably through winters, but, oh, those summers.

Extremes of heat create clear visible damage. In 1995 my garden suffered a three-day period of daily highs above 100 degrees. Shade plants fully sheltered were generally unharmed, but those hit by even small amounts of sun for a brief part of the day showed stress. *Hosta* (hosta or plantain lily) in partial shade sported large, gruesome patches of collapsed tissue that browned and finally crisped. Other plants suffered brown and curling edges on their foliage: *Dicentra spectabilis* (bleeding heart), *Astilbe* (false spirea), and *Thalictrum rochebrunianum* (meadow rue). *Alchemilla mollis* (lady's mantle) lay limp and gasping. *Lamium maculatum* 'White Nancy' (spotted deadnettle) had been beautiful in both shade and part sun, but with skyrocketing temperatures dehydrated and died back. Only *Lamium* plants in full shade survived to see the fall. *Digitalis* (foxglove) bloom stalks drooped (*D. x mertonensis* and *D. lutea*) or snapped in the middle (*D. purpurea*). Even tough, sun-loving *Hemerocallis* (daylily) plants, especially those on dry sites, showed streaky foliage damage.

Coping

To grow a beautiful flower garden in such a climate you need to be savvy. There are several things you can do to cope. Begin by knowing your USDA hardiness zone. This will tell you which perennial plants will survive the winter in your area. (Perennials are herbaceous—nonwoody—plants that live for several years. Some may die to the ground in winter, but the root survives to send up new growth in spring.) You live in zone 4 or 5. Check the map in the front of this book (or on the back cover) and engrave the number in your mind. Trustworthy catalogs will include a hardiness rating in each plant description. The rating is given as a range, such as 5–8, or as a single figure, such as 6. If your zone number is within the range given, then you can expect the plant to survive winter in your garden. When hardiness is noted as a single digit, it indicates the lowest (coldest) zone number in which a plant is winter hardy. If the single zone listed is 3, then the plant in question can withstand a winter a good deal colder than zone 5 and should breeze through an Iowa January. A 7 means the plant can handle a winter only as cold as the one dished out in zone 7, so zone 5 is definitely too cold.

Once you are an experienced gardener, you can try cheating by one zone. A zone 6 plant, not generally winter hardy in zone 5, might survive planted in a protected spot and given extra winter cover. You could put it against a stone wall, for instance, and apply mulch after the weather turns cold and the ground freezes. Generally, though, you can expect the best vigor, bloom production, and longevity from plants if you stick to your correct zone.

Always check the hardiness of a plant before you make a purchase. To supplement catalog information, you need a couple of good reference books that list perennials and include hardiness ratings. Take a look at the books listed in chapter 9 for suggestions. An English garden book edited for publication in the United States is not a good source of zone information. Unfortunately, some catalogs provide no hardiness rating. This irresponsible habit leads many a novice gardener astray. Not every thrillingly described plant in the listing is suitable for a Midwestern garden. Beware. Planting a perennial with a hardiness rating more than one zone warmer than your own guarantees failure. Don't throw your money away. Take the time to check.

To complicate matters, a second hardiness rating scheme, created by Arnold Arboretum, uses a slightly different numbering system. Though far less common than the USDA system, it does occasionally turn up, so find the map the book or catalog uses and double-check your zone.

Once you have selected a plant appropriate to your zone, the question remains, Will it handle the heat? Until very recently, there has been no heat-zone system comparable to the USDA hardiness zone map. However, in 1997, the American Horticultural Society (AHS) published its Plant Heat-Zone Map assigning zone numbers based on the number of days that temperatures are above 86 degrees. Following the AHS heat-zone scheme, your garden in the hot Midwest is most likely located in heat-zone 5 (thirty to forty-five days above 86 degrees) or heat-zone 6 (forty-five to sixty days above 86 degrees). This breakthrough in recognizing and quantifying the effect of heat on plants should in the long run make it easier to select appropriate specimens for your garden. Presumably nurseries will gradually begin to assign heat ratings to plants just as they now use cold hardiness zones. In some dreamy, utopian future the catalogs will tell you that the plant you're smitten with is cold hardy to USDA zone 5 and heat hardy to AHS heat-zone 6. The AHS suggests that plant listings in catalogs will give a rating such as "3–8, 8–1," showing cold hardiness zone range first, followed by heat-zone range. Check the AHS Plant Heat-Zone Map in the first color photo section of this book for your heat-zone.

Chapter 5 is an encyclopedia of flowering plants that thrive in our climate. The few weaklings included (because they're just too ravishing to omit) are clearly noted. For plants not listed, ask experienced gardeners in your area or consult a nursery professional— one you trust to be honest even when it means losing a sale. A plant's native habitat can also be a clue to the degree of success you can expect in heat. Obviously if it's native to mountain meadows it will sulk in scorching heat. Visit available local public gardens often to observe plant performance.

Plant in full sun are words bandied about loosely by garden writers who dwell in milder climes. In the hot Midwest you must take these words with a large grain of salt. Our full sun is glaring and very strong from mid-June to mid-September. Plants that bloom in the sweet, watery light of spring can be sited in full sun without fear. At that time the sun's rays are low, slanting, and gentle. However, plants that bloom in the more direct and damaging rays of midsummer should be given careful site consideration. Some garden books suggest, for example, planting hostas in sun. Any experienced Midwestern gardener can tell you this is folly.

Fortunately, many plants thrive in hot, direct sun. Even during an extended spell above 100 degrees some plants can be counted on to perform in full sun. *Calamintha nepeta* (lesser calamint), *Nepeta* (catmint), and *Perovskia atriplicifolia* (Russian sage) are completely unaffected by heat and drought, even without watering. *Coreopsis verticillata* 'Moonbeam' (threadleaf tickseed) remains very cool and beautiful in the worst summer heat. *Echinops ritro* (small globe thistle), *Achillea* (yarrow), daylilies, perennial varieties of *Aster, Boltonia asteroides, Rosa* (rose), Siberian irises, *Artemisia stelleriana* (beach wormwood), *Chrysanthemum, Echinacea* (coneflower), *Rudbeckia fulgida* var. *sullivantii* 'Goldsturm' (black-eyed Susan), *Verbascum* (mullein), and *Lilium lancifolium,* syn. *L. tigrinum* (tiger lily) are other examples of plants that can beat the heat and glaring sun. Many annuals, such as *Tagetes* (marigold), *Petunia,* and *Consolida* (larkspur) also flourish in sun.

Still, only the strongest plants can tolerate the full blazing Midwestern sun. Many will need some respite. The most important time to protect plants is afternoon, when the sun is fiercest. You can provide this protection by planting where a physical structure (house, shed, arbor, bench, etc.) or a tree, shrub, or large plant offers shade for some part of the afternoon. A garden on the east side of your house basks in full morning sun, but feels the relief of shade in the afternoon. A garden on the west side receives the same amount of sunlight daily, but the light is stronger (and plants must be tougher) because the garden is shaded in the morning and exposed in the afternoon when sun is most direct. The house gives plants in both gardens protection by reducing the amount of sunlight, but on the west side the protection is less.

A garden close against the north side of your home is somewhat shady all day. This space offers too much sun protection and should be reserved for shade-loving plants. A garden on the south side is hottest of all. In this sun-blasted location, you should put plants that thrive on heat and sun. It is possible, however, to create small areas of sun protection. A shrub or tall perennial within the bed will cast some afternoon shade on its neighbor to the east. A small tree planted on the west end of the bed can create an area of afternoon shade.

July and August

Fortunately your garden won't have to endure a string of days over 100 degrees every summer, even in the blazing Midwest. What you can count on, though, is that somewhere in July and August, possibly much of that period, temperatures will shoot up above 90, the humidity will rise, and the garden will seem faded, wilted, and uninviting. The sweetly fresh darling buds of springtime will be only a faint memory. In May and June your garden bursts with bloom from bulbs and perennials. The list of plants in bloom lengthens each week until the last of June, when flowering is at its peak. In the doldrums of July and August, the loveliest spring bloomers are gone and the fall bloomers have not begun. Nothing much new is happening, and many of the spring perennials that continue to bloom do so only fitfully by midsummer. *Aquilegia* (columbine), roses, yarrow, foxgloves, and *Heuchera* (coral flower or coral bells) are still blooming, but are decidedly over the hill. Heat is bleaching and desiccating much that remains. A few perennials stand up to the heat, but many wilt and refuse to stand upright. You arrive home from work to find the idea of strolling through a dull, limp garden in baking heat insupportable.

How can you make your garden enjoyable at the peak of summer? First, remember to plant lovely and varied foliage. If you do this at the outset, your garden will be attractive in spite of the sun's wilting and fading effect on bloom. Second, plant daylilies. Forget the old orange daylilies your grandmother grew. The modern cultivars are superior in every way. The colors run from an icy pale yellow that suggests white through pinks and melons and salmons to roses, lavenders, deep purples, and reds. A careful mix of these sun lovers can create a gloriously colorful garden in spite of color-fading heat. Third, add to the daylilies a mix of other perennials that thrive and glory in heat and glaring sun so that you build your garden on a framework of these hardy plants. The lavender blue of Russian sage mixes beautifully with the rich red purple of *Hemerocallis* 'Little Grapette.' It's a combination that would make even an English gardener envious, and both plants are tough as nails in our climate. Finally, maximize late summer bloom by planting annuals.

Annuals

If you've begun dipping into garden literature at all, you already know there's a certain cachet to calling yourself a perennial gardener. You get to look down upon those who raise only marigolds, *Zinnia,* and petunias and say sniffishly, "Oh, annuals." The assumption is that if you have the taste and knowledge to grow perennials, you need nevermore sully your hands with mere annuals.

I say baloney. In the blast furnace of a Midwestern summer, annuals are the ideal plants to fill gaps in the perennial border. Annuals live only one season, growing from seed to full size, flowering, and setting seed in just a few months. Many of them achieve their magnificent peak in July and August, just when perennials are taking a breather. Although most annuals will add no foliage interest, they are robust and reliable bloomers whose showy flowers pep up a sun-faded garden. Hot season annuals include marigolds; petunias; zinnia; *Centaurea cyanus* (bachelor's button); *Nicotiana* (tobacco plant); *Cleome* (spider flower); *Lobularia maritima*, syn. *Alyssum maritimum* (sweet alyssum); *Heliotropium* (heliotrope); *Borago officinalis* (borage); *Salvia farinacea* (mealycup sage); *Salvia splendens* (scarlet sage); *Salvia viridis*, syn. *S. horminum* (annual clary sage); *Scabiosa atropurpurea* (pincushion flower); and *Celosia* (cockscomb). *Anethum graveolens* (dill), an annual herb, with its lovely sulfur yellow spray of bloom, makes a good cut flower and is utterly unaffected by heat.

By combining these hot weather annuals with daylilies and other perennials that take the heat of July and August you can make a good showing. This mix will carry you through till fall, when temperatures drop (especially at night), and asters, chrysanthemums, *Boltonia asteroides, Buddleia davidii* (butterfly bush), *Solidago* (goldenrod), and other perennials come to the fore again. As a bonus, most of the splendid summer annuals will continue to provide color at least through September.

Don't assume that all annuals are tough, drought-tolerant sun lovers, however. A few are delicate butterflies that look really good only in the cool of autumn and may not thrive long enough to see that season. *Calendula officinalis* (pot marigold), *Clarkia* (also called *Godetia*), *Gerbera,* annual asters, and *Matthiola* (stock) are examples. In an unusually cool, rainy year, they may survive and perform nicely, but most years they will be less than you had hoped. I don't recommend any of these for a hot Midwestern garden, but if you must grow them, try giving them a bit of afternoon sun protection. *Antirrhinum* (snapdragon) is another faint-hearted annual, though planted early it may give some bloom in spring and fall, with poor bloom in between. Look for varieties that indicate they are heat tolerant and provide them with light shade in the afternoon.

Other annuals grow and flower quickly, finishing too early to be useful in filling the hot late summer gap in perennial bloom. Examples are *Viola* (pansy and Johnny-jump-up), *Lobelia, Nigella damascena* (love-in-a-mist), and *Papaver* (poppy). If you plant them, expect to enjoy them in spring and early summer only.

The cheater's way to fill late summer gaps requires advance planning. When you plant your garden in spring, you're bound to have a few spare annuals. It's a mystery of the gardening game that if you need four annuals to fill a spot, they will be sold only in six-packs. Pot up the extra annuals and grow them as container plants until holes open up when a plant dies, an early bloomer is cut back, or a mistake in spacing becomes an eyesore. Dig a hole. Tap an annual out of its pot. Pop it into the hole. Problem solved.

Two-Season Garden

Another way to deal with the fiercely hot summer is to focus on the spring and fall garden and let summer be a long vacancy. If you hate heat and spend little time in the garden at summer's peak, then this may be the best approach for you. As a bonus, it gives you a clear time to take your summer vacation without missing anything wonderful in the garden!

Every gardener's goal is a riot of bloom in spring, summer, *and* fall, but this is difficult to achieve over the very long growing season in our area. Because our season is so long, plants that bloom in overlapping profusion elsewhere may be solo performers here. A New York garden starts its bloom with *Galanthus nivalis* (common snowdrop) in March and ends it in September with asters. In eastern Nebraska the snowdrops begin in February and the asters last through October or even longer (consult the sequence of bloom list in chapter 8 for a detailed look at the order of bloom in our area). It's lovely to have a long growing season, but I occasionally yearn for the abundance that a compressed season offers.

Very few plants bloom in all three seasons. In general, you can get one season of bloom in a given space only by sacrificing the other two seasons in that same space. To some extent, of course, you can double up by underplanting with bulbs that go dormant after they bloom in spring. A viable garden design choice is to capitalize on spring bulbs to build a two-season garden. Here's how. First, make a conscious decision to sacrifice summer bloom to gain more space for spring and fall flowering. Then double up bloom over a considerable area by underplanting with spring bulbs. This achieves a garden that is reasonably full of bloom over perhaps three spring months and two fall months, with only a pair of summer months of slight bloom. For example, plant *Narcissus* (daffodil) among daylilies and perennial asters or common snowdrops at the foot of Russian sage.

If a full abandonment of the summer garden seems too rash, you can use just a handful of big showy summer bloomers to create a pleasant summer garden while still concentrating your bloom in the cooler parts of the year. For example, *Rudbeckia fulgida* var. *sullivantii* 'Goldsturm' is a heavy-blooming perennial whose brilliant gold flowers cover the plant in summer. A few of these black-eyed Susans scattered about could single-handedly create the illusion of a garden in bloom at the peak of summer heat. Emphasis on foliage combinations will also help to preserve an attractive garden when bloom is at a low point. By choosing spring and fall bloomers with interesting contrasts of form, foliage texture, and color—the blue of *Baptisia australis* (blue wild indigo, false indigo, or plains false indigo), the fresh green of *Paeonia* (peony), the silvery arched spears of Siberian irises, the fine texture of catmint, the bushy form of asters and chrysanthemums, the silver brocade of *Artemisia stelleriana* (beach wormwood), and the ghostly apparition of Russian sage—you could maintain an attractive summer garden while still reserving plenty of space for show-stopping spring and fall displays.

Using Your Head

Other ways to beat the heat of July and August are just common sense. If the heat is intolerable in late afternoon, why go out into it? Get up an hour early and do your gardening at 6:00 or 7:00 A.M. Even in the hottest part of summer, the heat doesn't become oppressive until somewhere between 9:00 and 10:00 A.M. Spend a pleasurable hour or two watering and deadheading in the cool and quiet morning. The garden is refreshed from the relatively cool night, colors glow in the angled early morning light, and you can enjoy a bit of serenity before going to work. After dinner spend another hour outdoors. The heat has begun to wane and the light is just right to show off color without cooking the gardener. I urge you to heed Noel Coward's warning: "Only mad dogs and Englishmen go out in the mid-day sun."

If you must garden between 10:00 A.M. and 5:00 P.M., wear a hat. You'll be surprised at how much cooler you will feel, and the protection it provides for your skin is vital. Use sunscreen, too, and wear long sleeves. Our Midwestern farmers are often victims of skin cancer. Avoid this and the leathery look of a lifetime of overexposure to the sun by covering up sensibly.

You can continue your commonsense approach to gardening by using the hottest part of summer to perform lighter tasks. Review your garden design and make plans for transplanting. Most of us are all too ready to get a shovel and move a plant the moment the idea strikes. In July and August it's just plain too hot, for gardener and plant alike. It is, however, the perfect time to mull over plans. You don't have to guess how much space plants will take once you move them, because they've reached full size. I commend high summer to you as the time to sit in the shade of a tree with a glass of iced tea and a plate of cookies, contemplating your garden and the changes you will make once the temperature drops to a more reasonable level.

2

Designing a Garden

Making a garden begins and ends with design. Whole books—lots of them—have been written on the subject, and I don't claim to adequately cover it here. After twenty years of shuttling plants from place to place around my garden, I am only just beginning to see it really take shape. I've known the basic precepts of garden design for years (having read lots of those books), but have only now begun to absorb them. Somehow the basics don't make as much sense when you read about them as they do when you stumble over them yourself through years of frustrating trial and error. I offer you here my idea of the most important fundamentals in the hope (probably vain) that you'll absorb and use them without having to make your own twenty years of mistakes.

Design is the most essential part of the garden-making process and the most difficult to learn. You can study design with diligence and learn its elements without ever achieving brilliance in assembling them. Beyond the basics, you need an artistic bent, the courage to express your own personality, and the wit and maturity to

recognize what that means. Though beautiful gardens are made by hand, it is in the eye of the artist that the best of them are created.

I am not among the artistically blessed, but then most of us aren't. When I began gardening in my twenties, I had visions of myself as a sweet young thing, surrounded by a lush and lovely garden, admired by all. It was several years before I realized that gardens are created over time and their craft acquired over many years. As the garden fills with plants and takes shape, the gardener acquires wrinkles. It takes time to shape a garden, but it's worth it, because the process is at least as rewarding as the product.

Know Your Plants

Look at your first ten years in the garden as a period of apprenticeship, a time to learn your craft, and especially a time to learn your plants. When it comes to putting plants together to form a garden, the standard and frequently repeated advice is to make a splash by grouping three or more of the same kind, because perennial borders are said to flow together best if you overlap big drifts of color. Beginners should forget that advice, the sooner the better. In the long run it may be true, but in the short run your primary goal is to become familiar quickly with a large variety of plants since only familiarity will allow you to use plants well in designing a beautiful and vigorous garden. You need to discover what does well for you and what you love. Forget about those groupings of three and just start with one of everything. If you grow thirty different plants you will know far more after three years than you will if you grow three each of ten plants. Over time you can remove the failures and propagate or divide the successes to create mass effects. Most plants by their nature increase in size and number. As they mature they can be divided again and again to make those massed groupings.

As you grow different flowers and gain knowledge about them, make it a point to learn their names. Each of them possesses both a scientific name, also called the Latin or botanical name, and (usually) a common name. To understand garden catalogs and books and other gardeners, you need to learn both. The scientific name is especially important because each plant has only one, while it may have two, three, or even more common names. The first word in the scientific name indicates the genus, the second word names the species (also called the species epithet or the specific epithet). The cultivar, which names a variety produced by cultivation, follows these and is usually enclosed in single quotation marks. Using *Pulmonaria saccharata* 'Mrs. Moon' as an example, *Pulmonaria* is the genus, *saccharata* the species, and 'Mrs. Moon' the cultivar. This plant's common name is lungwort.

Don't let an inability to pronounce Latin stand in your way. *Cleome,* a common annual, is widely pronounced KLEE-ome in my neck of the woods, though plant dictionaries say the correct pronunciation is klay-O-mee. Longer names like *Polygonatum odoratum* 'Variegatum' can be a trifle daunting, but just take them one syllable at a time and give it your best shot. It doesn't really matter whether you can rattle off the correct pronunciation. The person you're addressing is probably at least as unsure as you are yourself. The key is to remember the name with its associated plant and add both to your internal plant encyclopedia.

Remember the Big Picture

In England the term *garden* is applied to the entire landscape around a house. In the Midwest, we call this a *yard* and the flower beds within it our garden. In planning, take your cue from the English. Your property may contain a deck, a fence, gates, a trellis, a shed, and a compost area, in addition to the house and garage. Taken together these create a feel that affects your pleasure in the garden. That flower bed you want to add will not exist in a vacuum. It will be part of a defined space with structures and other plantings and will look best if you try to tie it somehow to its surroundings.

Let's say you plan to extend existing plantings to wrap around one end of a garage. Stop looking down at the space you intend to fill with plants. Instead look up at the overall picture. Perhaps the back of your house is nicely tied to earth by embracing shrubs, but the garage—added later—rises starkly from the surrounding lawn. You can make the garden you plan more attractive and improve the big picture by using shrubs around the garage to echo those around the house. These in turn will make a handsome backdrop for the flowers in your garden.

A board fence may seem a cold, dull background for a flower bed. Cover it with a vigorous *Clematis* or *Parthenocissus tricuspidata* (Boston ivy) and it blends nicely with the big picture—soft, green, and enclosing. A wall may seem unpleasantly hard until draped in green. A plain white garden shed can glare in the harsh Midwestern summer sun, attracting more attention than your loveliest flowers. Paint it sage green, pale gray, or some appropriate soft pastel to quiet it down. A deck needs something to take its edges off and give it a sense of connection to the ground it occupies. A handful of plants in containers, a few shrubs along the edges, accent plants at corners, a shady tree to overhang it can provide this.

As you begin to garden, recognize that the space you devote to flower beds is likely to grow larger. You may start with a little strip of petunias on each side of a walkway, but soon you will be thinking those beds would be very nice doubled in width and planted with a few perennials and bulbs. That's just the beginning. A very few years of flower gardening will leave you firmly convinced that less is more when it comes to lawns.

Consider how you would like your property to develop. Look at pictures in books and magazines to garner ideas. Try to analyze your reaction to other gardens. Why do you love this particular photo or that friend's garden? Is it the color scheme, the arrangement of the beds, the geometric layout, or the flowing curves? Probably the most usual sort of garden in the Midwest is one in which beds are laid out around the perimeter of the property and often against the house, too, leaving a swath of lawn between them. This can be attractive, but there are other approaches to consider. You might create island beds, plantings at sea within your lawn and unattached to architectural features. You could lay out geometrical beds with gravel paths. If you have plenty of space, you might even subdivide your yard into garden rooms, an approach popular on large properties in England. These separate areas, bounded by shrubs or walls, allow you to design several distinct gardens, each with its own color scheme and personality.

Anything added should be seen as a part of the big picture. Consider, of course, how a plant looks with its immediate neighbors, but don't forget the bigger view. How will it look when you sit down to supper in the garden and sweep your eye around? How will it fit into the whole procession when you look down the length of the garden? What view will it affect as you look out a window?

Present a Unified Front

If the front of a flower bed is unified, it does a lot to make the whole bed feel put together. This applies both to the edging material you use and to the plants placed along the front. Use of the same stone, brick, gravel, or wood chip path for edging throughout your yard will help to tie the whole thing together. Choosing the same brick or stone used in the construction of your home enhances that sense of unity.

Repetition of plantings at the front of a flower bed gives an impression of unity and flow. The sublime effect of a repeating edge can hardly be overstated. You don't need to place the same plant monotonously along the entire border or even confine yourself to three or four. The front of my large sunny border is edged with several different plants, but among them repetitions occur of *Heuchera* x *brizoides* 'Chatterbox' (coral flower or coral bells), *Coreopsis verticillata* 'Moonbeam' (threadleaf tickseed), and *Nepeta* x *faassenii*, syn. *N. mussinii* of gardens (catmint). The profusion of bloom on all three makes them showy, eye-catching plants, good choices for repetition. The catmint has soft bluish foliage with a flowing quality that speaks of romance, establishing the mood I want. Even when not in bloom, the distinctive foliage of all three plants gives the garden rhythm and sweep.

In my smaller shade border, just two dramatic patches of a variegated *Hosta* (hosta or plantain lily) give balance to a whole planting. Many other plants are mixed in along the front, but the repetition is what catches the eye. The white variegation in the dark shade stands out boldly. Typically, repetition is accomplished with two or more plants of the same kind, but you can also achieve it with plants of different kinds that have the same coloring. Since bloom occurs over only a fraction of a growing season, this works best with foliage color. In shade, for example, yellow-green *Lamium maculatum* 'Aureum,' syn. 'Gold Leaf' (spotted deadnettle) could echo a hosta of the same color. When you stand back, your eye catches the reiteration of color.

An ideal garden is full to bursting with shoulder-to-shoulder plants, but this doesn't always happen. In the real world, gardens sometimes have gaps where plants have died or failed to grow robustly. Maintaining close, full planting along the front edge is critical, because fullness here will disguise shortcomings elsewhere. Likewise, gaps here are much more likely to draw the eye.

Create Vistas

You can add great charm to your garden by providing something to look at across a distance. Paint a picture with a focal point toward which you will direct your eye. This can be as simple as placing a path so that a particularly beautiful tree lies at one end. You could also make a focal point of a statue or column, a birdbath or birdhouse mounted on a pole, a specimen plant, an arbor, a bench or chair, a gateway, an interesting urn or pot. If you don't have the perfect antique urn or specimen plant on hand, lay out the view anyway and trust time to provide it. Don't forget to look beyond your own garden. A flowering tree in your neighbor's yard, for instance, may feature strongly in your own garden vistas. I was reminded of this after a staggering winter storm damaged many trees in my city. A neighbor inquired anxiously whether the birch tree in my backyard would survive because it is a visually prominent part of her garden.

Provide a Background

The backdrop against which you see a flower bed can be a distraction or an asset. At the planning stage, you must see in your mind's eye not merely the flower bed, but also its setting. A garden is beautiful seen against the background of a stone wall. History and a rocky soil have provided these in abundance for gardeners in England and our own Northeast, but the Midwestern prairie doesn't cough up the raw materials required. Brick makes a nice substitute, but the cost is considerable. Shrubs form a lovely and lasting backdrop, making a garden seem natural and attached to the earth and giving it a strong vertical line.

If you decide to back your flower beds with shrubs, you'll need patience. They are slow growing compared to flowering perennials. The flowers may take three to five years to reach full size, but most shrubs will take more like eight to twelve. Notice shrubs in the gardens you visit. Look for them in catalogs and examine them at your local nursery. Hardiness zones of shrubs refer to the survival of the woody plant, not to the blooms, so it's worth inquiring whether the shrub flowers reliably in your area before you buy. Be especially cautious about plants that bloom on "old wood." This refers to bloom that occurs on the part of the plant that grew in the previous season. If winter creates dieback, you won't see flowers in spring.

As soon as you know what you want and where, get those shrubs in the ground. You'll be rewarded in a few years with a garden blessed with an established and comfortable charm. Early planting of shrubs offers the added advantage of preventing unwise plantings of perennials too close to fences or property lines. It's vital to determine the mature size of shrubs and space them accordingly. A natural tendency is to place them too close together, which achieves an immediate filled-in look, but leads to trouble in a few years when the shrubs begin to crowd one another. Resist the temptation to place large perennials or bulbs in the space between young bushes and encroach upon their growing space. Until the shrubs mature you can dress up overly open areas with annuals or small, easily moved perennials.

Shrubs can be used to create a look of formality when planted in rows to form a hedge and clipped to create straight lines. When planting hedges to create visual pathways, it's essential to know the ultimate size of the shrubs because placing them too closely in their infancy can make an unpleasantly claustrophobic walkway in the future. When in doubt, err on the side of roominess. For informality, try unclipped shrubs. If this is the look you strive for, give them plenty of room, because overcrowding will eventually demand regular pruning.

You can use individual shrubs to create interest in the background of a flower bed or in the bed itself if they are small. *Daphne* x *burkwoodii* 'Carol Mackie' is a small, slow-growing shrub with a variegated leaf and a neat dome shape. It makes a handsome addition to a flower bed and brings light to the shady setting it prefers. Shrubs with yellowish leaves or purple foliage make for nice contrast. Many shrubs can add the dimensions of flower and scent, too.

If your house is part of a garden's background, keep in mind its color. An amazing number of gardeners forget that the house is even in the picture. They fall in love with a shocking magenta rhododendron at the nursery and plant it smack in front of an orange brick house. Or they put a maple at the corner of a house painted mauve, forgetting that in fall the tree will be fiery red and orange. Or they bank the front of their white house with shrubs that bloom in ivory, looking shabby and dirty against their background. The true garden fanatic can always paint a wood house to complement favorite flowers, but if your home is brick or stone, you really do need to stop and think before planting.

Adhere to a Color Scheme

Color scheme is even more important in the garden than it is in your wardrobe, because a great part of your garden wardrobe is on display all at once. To create a sense of unity, pick a color scheme and stick to it. This is surprisingly hard to do. Color is intoxicating and so hugely appealing that I can't imagine choosing just one favorite color. Common color schemes discussed in garden literature are yellow and blue (or purple); white and gray (like Vita Sackville-West's famous White Garden); and pink, white, and blue (said to be English in flavor). There's nothing to stop you, though, from choosing some offbeat scheme to your own liking, say red and gray, or even red and orange. Your garden should be a reflection of the colors you love.

My own first choice color scheme is lots of pink in various shades, along with white and blue, pepped up with lemon yellow in small doses. I use gray foliage to emphasize the soft pastel look. *Crocosmia* 'Lucifer' sings me a siren song with its sharp, hot red, and only by self-discipline and constantly reminding myself that it would be hideous in my color scheme can I resist it. When it comes to color, you must focus. You can't have everything in life, so decide on a color combination and stick with it. If it's red, orange, and gold, you can't go messing about with lavender, pink, and lemon yellow. Satisfy your need for pastels by admiring other people's gardens. Focus on your color scheme whenever you acquire plants, even as gifts. The big difficulty here is that with most of us, taste develops over time. What appeals to you as a neophyte gardener may not as you mature, so your color scheme may shift over the years. This is one reason that mature gardens take so long to form.

It is possible in the Midwest for a single garden to have two color schemes, divided by season. A pastel color scheme of pink, white, blue, and yellow is easy to achieve in spring, but more difficult in the heat of Midwestern summer. A shift to gold, orange, and red might be desirable at that point. In the Midwest this is not as tricky as it sounds because the growing season is very long and a natural pause occurs between spring and summer bloom somewhere around the first of July. When the heat of summer strikes, spring bloomers step hastily aside.

Choosing plants by color descriptions can be confusing, because there is no common understanding of what exact shade any color word describes. A plant described as blue may be anything from royal blue or aquamarine to pale lavender or purple. Capturing flower colors on film is a tricky business, too, so even scrutiny of catalog photos may not help. If you make a habit of looking carefully at plant colors (both leaf and flower) in nurseries, your friends' gardens, and in your own flower beds, you can gradually build up a knowledge of plant color to aid you in garden design. When you choose a color scheme, be clear with yourself about whether you want sky blue or purple or lavender or aquamarine. Then compare book and catalog descriptions and ask experienced gardeners for advice.

As you fine-tune your garden design, you'll probably wind up moving just about every plant at least once. Try to make the decision about a plant's final destination while it is still in bloom. Color memory is surprisingly short, so making a good decision is much easier when you directly compare a plant's blossoms with those of its prospective neighbors.

Unfortunately for your color design, the heat and glaring sunlight of a sunny location in our region dramatically change colors. The sun makes them *appear* faded and the heat fades them *in fact* as well as in appearance. I first became aware of this phenomenon when I visited my sister-in-law's garden in Minneapolis. She cut a handful of annuals for a small bouquet and I was swept away by their jewel-like colors. I particularly recall the luscious tangerine of her *Calendula officinalis* (pot marigold). This was an annual I had never seen before, and based on the brilliant loveliness of hers, I grew some myself the following year, only to be disappointed by their comparatively dull orange. Both in my garden and in bouquets their color lacked the freshness, life, and clarity I remembered. The heat and sun of southeastern Nebraska had sapped the color's vitality. For beautiful color in the hot Midwest, it's best to stick with plants that can handle heat and to bear in mind when selecting colors that the glaring sun will wash them out.

To do a good job of planning, you need to notice colors. It's very easy to err horribly in choosing garden companions because you overlook what is right under your nose. Not all whites, for example, are pure bridal white. Many are really ivory or off-white with a pink or yellow cast. Planting white next to off-white forms an unpleasant combination; the less white plant looks tawdry. *Convallaria* (lily-of-the-valley) planted next to *Tiarella wherryi,* syn. *T. cordifolia* var. *collina* (Wherry's foamflower) is a classic mistake in this department. The lily-of-the-valley is too snowy for the foamflower's cream blushed with dusty pink. Whites (as opposed to creams and ivories) look pure and sweet in the soft sunlight of spring, but seem to glare unpleasantly in the harsh light of summer in the hot Midwest. In early May *Iberis sempervirens* (candytuft) is wonderful in masses, but a month later, in the more direct sun of a later season, white irises and daisies strike the eye keenly and are more attractive used sparingly. You may think of white as a noncolor, but in fact it is a very strong and eye-attracting color in both bright sunlight and shade. In the darkness of shade, this is a desirable quality. Masses of white can lighten a dark place. Just as you wear white when you go for a walk at night so that you are visible to drivers, you can dress your shade garden in white to create visibility.

Plants called "yellow" are often gold instead, and the two do not suit the same color schemes. Gold—an orange shade of yellow—is gorgeous with reds and oranges and purples. However, if you're looking for a dash of yellow to spice up a pastel color scheme, you want yellow green, sulfur, lemon yellow, or perhaps butter yellow, but definitely not gold. Gold stands up very well in brilliant sunlight, while the yellows are somewhat paled by it. *Rudbeckia fulgida* var. *sullivantii* 'Goldsturm' (black-eyed Susan) is a strong perennial whose brilliant gold color never flinches in full sun or heat wave.

Yellow and gold are not happy companions in the garden. One or the other may suit your color plan, but probably not both. Having said that you don't want to put yellows with golds or whites with creams, I should mention the exception. You can make these combinations work if you choose a monochromatic (one-color) scheme. For instance, if you decide on a white garden, you can combine all of the whites—from the purest most blinding white to the creams and even very faint pinks—because the contrasts are dulled by the sheer number of shades. The eye is confused by profusion into seeing a whole instead of individual pairings. It's like looking at a multiple-hued print fabric: you don't notice whether individual colors within the print clash because you see only the colorful whole. If you're mad about the yellow color range, you can create an all-yellow garden using everything from pale butter yellow to the brashest gold.

Flowers described as "blue" are nearly always a shade of purple. Truly sky blue flowers are few in number. Rarest of all is that sumptuous shade of brilliant blue found in *Myosotis alpestris* (alpine forget-me-not) and *Brunnera macrophylla,* syn. *Anchusa myosotid-iflora* (Siberian bugloss). Nature is much more lavish with the violets, purples, and lavenders that are typically called blue in garden catalogs: *Nepeta* (catmint), *Campanula* (bellflower), *Viola* x *wittrockiana* (pansy), irises, asters, *Phlox divaricata* (woodland phlox or wild sweet William), *Baptisia australis* (blue wild indigo, false indigo, or plains false indigo).

"Pink" is used to describe a great range of shades from pale pink or lavender to a vivid, eye-assaulting hot pink. The latter, sometimes described as fuchsia or magenta, is a jolt of color that can perk up a wan pastel color scheme even in very small shots. Magenta is sometimes disparaged as too bright to be easily mixed with other colors. However, this is not a concern in the hot Midwest, where the glare of summer's sun seems to drain away color. Here magenta's brilliance is rather to be sought out than avoided. The paler pinks can become insipid in the blinding light of July and August. Dashes of magenta will enliven them.

Red, gold, orange, and purple can show some oomph in the glare of fierce sunlight. In a climate of milder sunshine they might seem garish, but here they make a warm and cheerful summer color scheme. Certain vividly colored flowers, however, fade under direct sun. I'm speaking here not of a perceived lessening of color caused by excessive light, but of a real sapping of color in heat and full sun. *Hemerocallis* (daylily) is the most obvious example. Some red and purple cultivars fade dramatically unless placed in partial shade.

Gray foliage is actually a pale, soft green, usually with fuzzy leaves that add to the impression of softness. This gray green strikes me as a very relaxing, calming color. It cools and offers pleasant contrast to darker greens. It may have a blue or yellow cast, which you may want to take note of when combining grays.

The Importance of Foliage

Nearly everything you read on garden design will emphasize the importance of foliage. You were probably drawn to gardening in the first place because you love flowers, so you're thinking, phooey on foliage. I once felt the same, but after several years of gardening I've changed my tune. Let me try to convince you of the essential importance of foliage.

Many perennials flower for only one to three weeks, and even those considered long-blooming usually flower for only about six weeks. In zone 5, the garden is in bloom and under scrutiny from February when the *Crocus* bloom until the last asters freeze in October or even November—around thirty-five weeks. Deduct just a couple of weeks for zone 4. This leaves you plenty of time to contemplate the unadorned foliage of even your favorite long bloomers. The phrase *nonstop bloomer* is a fiction of nursery catalogs. No perennial blooms profusely from spring through to fall. That's why leaves are so significant. If foliage is graceful, glossy, fuzzy, silvery, unusually colored, variegated, textured, or exceptionally large or tiny, it introduces dimension and interest to your garden. The satisfying leafy tapestry you weave with it is fresh and beautiful for most of the growing season.

Some wonderful bloomers have uninteresting leaves. The daylily is a prime example. Planting daylilies in masses will make a very dull picture for the many weeks during which they do not bloom. Certainly you don't want to eliminate every plant from your list whose foliage is ho-hum, but you do need to take into consideration all shortcomings. If a plant's foliage is boring, place it in small groupings among plants with handsomer or simply different foliage. The big, straplike green leaves of daylilies are lackluster in masses, but can be contrasted with the rounded leaves of *Heuchera* (coral flower or coral bells), the diminutive leaves of *Calamintha nepeta* (lesser calamint), or the silvery leaves of *Stachys byzantina,* syn. *S. lanata* (lamb's-ears) to create appeal.

Seek plants whose foliage is attractive to your eye. Watch for color, texture, and size that can provide contrast in a scene of unrelenting smooth dark green. Consider planting *Hosta sieboldiana* var. *elegans* for the dramatic effect of its massive leaves, in spite of its unimpressive bloom. Don't worry that shade-loving *Athyrium niponicum* (Japanese painted fern) will never bloom at all; its delicate frosty fronds are reward enough.

On a visit to the garden of a professional horticulturist, I swept my eye over an attractive perennial border and realized what did not at first strike me about the scene: relatively few plants were in bloom. The designer had used varying kinds of foliage—particularly variegated foliage—to produce enduring texture, movement, and interest in the garden. At a different season, masses of bloom would be the frosting on the cake, but this cake was quite satisfying without the frosting.

Make a Plan

It's useful to plan a garden on paper before planting it. Use graph paper with quarter-inch squares and let each square represent a square foot. Measure your existing or planned bed and outline it on graph paper. You can then pencil sketch your plants onto the design, leaving appropriate space for each. A plant that grows thirty-six inches wide will need a space three squares by three squares. You can sketch and erase till you get it right or you can use cutouts. Cut shapes to represent plant sizes out of a different sheet of graph paper. Label them with plant names, then push them around on your garden outline till you're happy with the result. If you like, spray the back of the cutouts with Photo Mount (available at photo shops) before cutting. This makes them tacky enough to stay put in a draft, but they can still be moved around easily.

Putting things on paper lets you stand back and take a look. This is the time to notice that you've put two yellow-blooming plants side by side or plants with very similar foliage too close together. You may also discover that the space where you contemplated putting sixteen plants has room for only eight or that you've planned too many different varieties for your space.

Getting your garden on paper helps you to visualize and think things through. Mistakes can be fixed with an eraser instead of a shovel. A plan on paper is especially useful for beginning and intermediate gardeners who have trouble keeping all the attributes of each plant straight: plant height, width, shape, sun or shade requirements, moisture needs, height of bloom, bloom color, foliage color, foliage shape and texture, bloom shape and form. It's a lot to juggle mentally. A picture helps. As you become more knowledgeable you'll find you can keep all these factors in mind and design more directly in the garden, but it still helps to think the entire design through before you pick up a shovel. It's also a great boon to have a plan on paper when midwinter rolls around. This is when your memory of exact plants and locations is getting dim and you're looking at nursery catalogs, ready to order plants for next year.

Please the Eye

Beyond the flower color and foliage of individual plants, there's plenty that goes into the formation of a pleasing garden picture. A garden is most beautiful when viewed down its length. From this perspective, an illusion of fuller bloom is created by the magic of foreshortening. Empty spots disappear. The garden is especially lovely with the evening light behind it. If you can site your bed so that you see down its length with the setting sun behind it, grab the opportunity. This garden will run east and west lengthwise with your viewing point on the east side, looking west. As the sun angles low in the sky, the flower petals will become stained glass, their jewel colors breathtakingly vivid. If you spend more time in your garden in the morning, reverse the layout to catch the rising sun.

Without constant attention to vertical line in plants, you are likely to find yourself always looking down on a planting about as interesting as wall-to-wall carpet—uniformly low and dull. The occasional *Lilium* (lily), *Verbascum* (mullein), *Thalictrum rochebrunianum* (meadow rue), or *Delphinium* brings the garden up to eye level and adds elegance. Roses, *Buddleia davidii* (butterfly bush), tall perennial asters, *Cleome* (spider flower), and other sizable plants give height, substance, and form. To add interest, vary not only the height of plants but also their general shape. Spikes, clumps, ground huggers, fans, bushy shapes, and so on should mix it up to provide movement. Do the same with bloom size and shape.

For a casual cottage garden look, use annuals and short-lived perennials that self-seed in an unplanned way to fill gaps and soften the overall look: *Consolida* (larkspur), *Viola tricolor* (Johnny-jump-up), *Lychnis coronaria* (rose campion), *Aquilegia* (columbine), *Borago officinalis* (borage). Use weavers—those that spread gradually to close up spaces and work in around their neighbors—to fill in the picture. For this tapestry effect use *Nepeta* (catmint), *Coreopsis verticillata* 'Moonbeam' (threadleaf tickseed), *Lamium maculatum* (spotted deadnettle), *Veronica prostrata* (prostrate speedwell), *Mazus reptans, Artemisia stelleriana* (beach wormwood), *Astilbe chinensis* var. *pumila* (false spirea), or *Galium odoratum,* syn. *Asperula odorata* (sweet woodruff).

Plan ahead to disguise plants not in bloom. Irises make sizable plants that bloom for a brief time, after which the foliage is all too likely to be attacked by disease. Plant irises among daylilies, whose attention-catching blooms come on just as the irises are looking their worst. I grow *Leucanthemum vulgare,* syn. *Chrysanthemum leucanthemum* (ox-eye daisy), a legacy from a previous gardener. In flower the daisies are classic white, but after bloom the foliage becomes rank. I plant my ox-eyes among asters that don't begin to grow large until about the time the daisies fade. I cut back the daisies when the flowering ends and let the asters take over. Obviously all this camouflage is unnecessary when a plant's leaves are beautiful on their own.

If the bad traits of a plant simply can't be disguised, then you must follow an important basic precept of garden design: be ruthless! Your garden will have failures—plants that simply don't perform well. Weak growth or a flopping habit or a color that doesn't quite suit or some other character flaw will cause the plant to seriously disappoint you. Some of these shortcomings may be remedied by maturity, but if you have had a perennial in your garden for three years and still it lets you down, show no mercy. Dig it up and pitch it. This can be unexpectedly difficult to do. You find yourself thinking of the poor old thing as a breathing personality and feel almost as if you are tossing a puppy on the rubbish heap. You must be firm. Take no prisoners. Out it goes. Until you are able to do this your garden will be so full of unsuccessful or second-rate plants that you will have no hope of producing the lovely artistic whole toward which you strive.

In laying out your garden don't forget to give yourself a place to sit down and enjoy it. A bench placed where you can sit in the shade and admire your creation can greatly enhance your delight. Consider at what time of day you are most likely to sit down to contemplate your little paradise and site the bench so that you will not be blinded or baked by sunlight at that hour. A spot for outdoor dining is another very good idea. In the spring and fall when weather is cool and pleasant, nothing is more restful than dinner in the garden. Time seems to stand still as you relax without effort.

3

Dirt

This should have been chapter 1, but frankly, I didn't want to scare you off. Fixing your soil is the first step to a good garden. It's also hard work that many of us would like to avoid. When you paint a house, you start by cleaning and scraping, even though you'd just as soon bypass this arduous and uncreative phase. After a few hours of the tedious stuff, you're finally able to pick up a paintbrush. It's the same in the garden. After a few hours of loosening and amending your soil, you're ready to get creative with the plants. Most beginning gardeners want a yard full of blooms to spring magically from the unaltered earth at their feet. It's not going to happen. Even if you've been gardening for a few years, you may still be trying to scrape by with little or no soil preparation. You need to get serious about giving your perennial plants the rich, loose, moist, fertile soil they deserve.

Sand and Clay

Start with the dirt right under your feet. Unless you have moved onto a property that was formerly owned by a really good gardener, your soil is probably nothing to brag about. If it is sandy, you already have the good drainage that many desirable perennial plants demand. Your soil is easy to work with—loose, light, and gritty. What you lack is the humus (partially decayed vegetable matter) that will supply nutrients and increase moisture retention. Water runs so freely through sandy soil that nutrients wash away quickly and the soil will be dry. The sandy particles hold heat, too, making the soil hotter in warm months and contributing to its dryness.

Many of us in the Midwest are up against clay soil. Clay is solid and heavy. It is difficult to get through with a shovel, hard to lift and turn, sticky when wet, and iron hard when dry. It is a knee-wrecking, backbreaking misery to work with and inhospitable to the many plants that require good drainage. Water soaks into clay soil slowly, making it difficult to water adequately without causing runoff. On the other hand, clay soil is moisture retentive and rich in nutrients. Whining is a favorite pastime of gardeners who must till the clay. No matter how awful your own soil may be, other gardeners will triumphantly insist that theirs is worse. One gardener I know even made a little bowl out of the clay in his garden just to prove its nasty nature.

Whether you're dealing with clay or sand, you can improve it dramatically by adding organic material in generous amounts. This added humus will make clay easier to dig. Plant roots will penetrate more easily and the soil will be more free draining. Sandy soil, improved with humus, will drain more slowly, retain moisture, and have better structure and body. More nutrients will be available and they will leach away more slowly.

Compost

The very best way to add organic material to your soil is to dig in plenty of compost. Compost makes a lovely, healthy garden possible. There are so many ways to use it that you will never truly have enough. Although you may be able to buy this magical ingredient at a local garden shop or even get it free from a municipal composting operation, your best bet for an economical and reliable supply of good quality compost is to make it in your own backyard.

If you start in May, you can have usable compost by September. This may seem like a long time, but the point is that it will be September whether you start composting now or not. If you get moving, it can be September *with compost.*

You may be dragging your feet because you've been taken in by all the detailed baloney about the Science of Composting. Well, you can forget about thermometers, expensive bins, lids, ideal siting, ideal ratios. Composting is really very simple. After all, it's perfectly natural for organic material to rot. All you have to do is speed the process along. Here's how.

Begin by deciding how you'll contain your compost heap. There are various kinds of bins on the market, and garden literature offers plans for building bins. You don't absolutely need a bin at all. You can just pile your materials on the ground. If you choose to use a bin, the type you select probably won't significantly affect the speed with which you turn out compost or the quality of the final product.

I use two kinds of bins. The first is a heavy-duty three-bin beauty my husband built me to the specifications of James Underwood Crockett in *Crockett's Victory Garden* (Boston: Little, Brown, 1977). It is a masterpiece of solid craftsmanship, but it doesn't make compost one whit better than do my other bins, purchased at a local hardware store. They were relatively inexpensive and a snap to assemble. Each bin consists of four sides of coated wire grid held together by four metal skewers that stabilize the bin simply by sticking into the ground. The green wire filled with green and brown materials blends into the garden scene far less obtrusively than the big three-bin job that had to be constructed by someone with building skills. With the wire grid bins it's quick and easy to add another bin, take one down to store, and take the front off to turn the pile.

Siting your pile in a sunny spot will warm it and probably speed the rotting process. Most of us, though, will opt for a hidden location under trees or behind shrubs, where composting will work perfectly well, even if a bit more slowly.

Pay attention now: this paragraph is as technical as I'm going to get. Compost requires just four ingredients: oxygen, water, and two kinds of organic material—carbon-rich and nitrogen-rich. Carbon-rich materials are tough and fibrous, like tree leaves, thick plant stalks, and straw. Nitrogen-rich materials are soft, like grass clippings, fruit and vegetable peelings, garden trimmings, and manure.

Once you've got your containers in place, start filling one of them with carbon-rich materials and nitrogen-rich materials. Simply alternate six-inch layers of the two types. If you use a layer of manure, it will be very high in nitrogen and can be thinner—an inch or two. If the materials you add are dry, sprinkle on a little water, but don't overdo it, because you don't want a sodden mass that squashes oxygen out of the pile.

There is no precise recipe for what you put in the pile. Use grass clippings, trimmings from the garden, fruit and vegetable peelings, horse or cow manure, and tree leaves. Any nonwoody vegetable matter is fine. Steer clear of moldy or diseased plant materials and weed seeds. House pet waste may carry disease and should be avoided. Never put meat, fish, grease or cooking oil, or bones in your compost: you may attract wild animals, including rats.

Oxygen maintains aerobic activity. Without it, rotting slows down and the pile stinks. Keep the oxygen level high by turning the pile every six or eight weeks during the warm season. In cold weather the pile doesn't rot so there's no reason to turn it. The hotter the weather, the faster the pile will rot and the sooner it can be turned.

Work toward making a pile about four feet high and four feet across, but you don't have to build your pile all at once. Just add to the pile as you have materials available. When you put in edibles like kitchen trimmings, cover them with a layer of grass clippings, dirt, or leaves to prevent odors. Sprinkle on a bit of water as you go if the pile seems dry. When the pile reaches four feet high, turn it over. Use a pitchfork to make the work easy. If you have more than one bin, turn the pile into a new bin and start another pile where the first one was. In six or eight weeks you'll have the new pile finished. Then you can move both piles to new bins and start a third heap. About the time the third pile is ready to turn, your first pile will be ready to use.

When the autumn leaves begin to fall they make lovely compost, too. Just use them as a high carbon layer in your regular compost pile. Oak leaves, however, are very tough and slow to break down, so I don't add them to my regular piles unless they are finely chopped. Instead, I make separate oak leaf bins alternating with grass clippings for finished compost in about eighteen months. It may seem like a long time to wait, but the leaves make terrific compost.

Your piles will decompose faster if you chop the materials you add. Cut them up with clippers, run them through a mulcher/shredder (not a chipper, which is designed to chop small branches), or run over them with a mulching mower. You can also hasten breakdown by adding manure, so do that if you have a free supply. Cow manure is ideal. Commercial compost starters or high nitrogen fertilizers can also be used to speed decomposition. The real beauty of compost, though, is that you can make this miraculous product without spending a lot of money. Buy a pitchfork and three bins and you're in business. Everything else you need is free, and if money is really short, you don't absolutely have to have the bins either.

Finished compost is often described as brown and finely crumbled, like chocolate cake crumbs. Don't worry if yours doesn't get that fine. You have usable compost when it has an overall blended, crumbly look, with relatively few distinguishable stems and leaves.

If most of it is crumbly you don't need to worry about a few pieces as big as three or four inches across. The rotting process will continue after you add the compost to your garden. If any of the pieces seem too large, just toss them back onto your newest pile and let them decompose more thoroughly.

Once you've made your first bin of compost, you can start digging it into your soil to improve texture, moisture retention, and drainage. Light, sandy soil will mix easily with the compost, but if you have clay soil, there's one more step to take.

Loosen Clay Soil with Gypsum

You need to mix lots of compost into clay to improve drainage and create a friable soil for plant roots, but mixing anything into the sticky mass of clay is no small chore. You must first break the clay up into smaller particles that will mix more easily with organic materials. You can soften the soil by watering it well the day before you plan to dig it over. If it is still too hard, you can loosen clay soil with gypsum.

Gypsum, available in bags at nurseries, is a powdery or grainy mineral that can work miracles on clay soil. If you've tried it already without success, you probably haven't used it properly. You can't simply sprinkle it over the surface. It must be worked in along with compost. Every time you turn soil and hit heavy clay, sprinkle on gypsum and dig it in. If the clay is so solid that mixing in gypsum is very difficult, do the best you can, then water it in. The next day dig over the area again. It should be much easier to handle. As you work with gypsum, you'll find that the clay begins to break down from solid slabs into smaller, faceted bits.

Notice that I didn't tell you how much gypsum to add. Neither does the bag it comes in, and I've never seen a formula suggested. It all depends. Let's say you're digging a gallon-size hole. Try adding a quarter cup of gypsum and two shovels full of compost. Mix it all up and water it. Come back the next day to dig it over again. Was it enough? You're going for a soil loose enough to allow you to add liberal amounts of compost. Just experiment. It shouldn't take long to get the feel of it. The more solid the clay, the more gypsum you need. Gypsum will work its magic over a period of time. You'll see some initial improvement, followed by great improvement over a few months.

It's a good idea to go slowly when using gypsum because it can raise the pH level of your soil, making it more alkaline. Since most perennials like a slightly acid pH, your garden will not thrive if the soil becomes too alkaline. Add gypsum gradually and have your soil tested periodically to avoid problems. Check with your cooperative extension service office to find out where to get a soil test.

Using Compost

The quickest and most efficient way to improve your soil is to prepare a bed before you plant anything. Obviously, your only chance to do this is when you first plant the bed.

Many garden books suggest double digging. This involves digging a trench twenty to twenty-four inches deep. You then put the turf you removed from the surface upside down in the bottom of the hole to rot. The relatively rich top soil goes on top of it. Over this you shovel the poorer bottom soil. This effectively reverses the soil, putting the richest soil at the bottom to feed the roots. For a modest five-foot-by-ten-foot bed this would require moving one hundred cubic feet of soil twice—once to take it out, once to put it back. You may wish to contemplate this if you have light, sandy soil and the back of an ox, but if you are gardening on clay, the whole idea is laughable.

You don't need to suffer through the amount of brute labor required for double digging. You can provide plants with a reasonable amount of root space in loose soil by what I call single digging.

Loosen and turn the soil to the depth of one shovel plunged well down into the earth. You'll be going down somewhat less than a foot. If you are working with clay soil, add gypsum. Now layer on compost and dig the bed over again, breaking it up and mixing in the gypsum and compost. Ideally your layer of compost would be four to five inches thick, but realistically this amount may not be available. Use what you can lay your hands on. Your city may have a community composting center you can tap. If you're wealthy and have the good sense to spend your money on something really valuable, buy some compost at your local nursery.

If compost isn't available for sale locally and your own compost heap hasn't yet started producing, consider buying sphagnum peat moss. Peat moss is an organic soil amendment available in bales at the nursery. Oddly enough, this material, which is extremely moisture-retentive once moist, is also very difficult to moisten once it becomes thoroughly dried out. Lay your bale on its side, cut open the broad top, and water it. Hot water will be absorbed much more readily than cold. The first water out of a sun-warmed hose on a hot day is good. I sometimes heat water in a teakettle to add along with hose water. One word of caution about peat moss: large amounts of it can make the whole soil difficult to moisten once dried. Compost is definitely preferable when available.

The addition of all this organic matter and the digging and loosening of the soil will raise the level of the bed a few inches, so that between the depth you've dug down and what you've added, you now have rich, loose soil at least a foot deep. This is enough to make just about any perennial very happy. If you've planned ahead, you can dig the bed in the fall and let the freezing and thawing of winter thoroughly mix all of your ingredients for a beautiful soil texture come spring.

Unfortunately, you may be dealing with a flower garden *already established* in unprepared soil. If your bed is already planted and you can't dig and enrich the whole thing at once, it is possible to fix your soil piecemeal. This takes time, but ultimately will result in lovely, loose, rich garden soil. Every time you plant or transplant, loosen the soil thoroughly a full shovel deep, add gypsum if you're working with clay, and enrich the soil with compost. Be especially generous with the compost if you are planting something that likes moisture and rich soil.

In the fall, put a layer of compost over your entire garden—two to four inches. Hoe it lightly into the surface, avoiding roots. Even without any digging, the compost somehow softens and mixes with the soil over the winter.

You can also mulch your beds with compost in the spring to retain moisture and discourage weeds. This works well to give new plants a start, babying them along till their root systems are big enough to weather a bit of drying. About an inch of compost will do it. I don't recommend a thicker layer because it seems to keep moisture out as well as it holds it in. If the compost layer is too thick, thorough watering will moisten its surface without penetrating to the soil beneath it. If you want to add more compost in spring than just an inch, be sure it is well rotted and fine textured. Then hoe it in lightly to blend it with the soil surface while being careful not to damage plant roots. If you find yourself short on compost, *do not* substitute peat moss as a mulch, because it will dry out and prevent moisture from penetrating.

Even enriched loose soil will tend to compact on the surface after a hard rain or following a dry spell. Use a hoe to loosen the surface so that water can penetrate easily. Be careful not to pile compost or any other mulch directly against plant stems. Mulch *around* plants, not *over* them. Allowing mulch materials to crowd against stems or cover foliage will cause the plant to rot and may kill it. Never mulch tall bearded irises, as they like to have their rhizomes (rootstocks) right at surface level.

Routine use of compost (and gypsum on clay) will build and maintain a ravishing garden soil. Apply a heavy layer of compost on new beds, moderate compost in fall, and a thin compost mulch in spring. Add compost in every hole you dig as you plant and transplant. You will notice an immediate improvement in your soil. At the end of three years the difference will be stunning. The quality and texture of your soil will make you the envy of other gardeners, and every time you go out into your garden you will hear a chorus of plants singing, "Thank you, thank you, thank you!"

What about Fertilizer?

If you are considering buying a fertilizer for your flower beds, take a look at the three numbers prominently displayed on the label that indicate the chemical content, such as 5-10-5 or 0-10-10. The first number represents nitrogen, which encourages fast, vigorous leafy growth. Because perennials are slow growing, nitrogen is not needed in quantity. The second number represents phosphorous, which promotes strong roots and stems and encourages flowering. The third number stands for potassium, which makes plants disease resistant. Choose a fertilizer with a low first number and a relatively high second number. If your soil is sandy, it may be potassium deficient, making the third number important.

If you feel you need commercial fertilizer, follow the instructions printed on the container. More is not better. More fertilizer than the package recommends may burn roots and can even kill your plants, especially young ones. Read the instructions and follow them to the letter.

I used to apply fertilizer each spring and was never really happy with the results. Finally one year a nursery employee told me that she used only bonemeal and compost and no commercial fertilizer at all. I tried it, liked it, and have seldom used a bag of fertilizer since. Bonemeal is high in phosphorous, that vital ingredient that encourages bloom and strong root and stem growth. It is slow acting compared to commercial fertilizer. In addition to adding compost and gypsum to my clay soil, I also dig in bonemeal each time I dig a hole. I add about a quarter cup for a small plant, about a half cup for a medium plant, and about one cup for a large plant like a shrub. When I prepare a new bed I sprinkle bonemeal over the entire bed, using the ratio stated on the package, and dig it in.

In the spring, I also like to add composted cow manure, except on plants that prefer a poor soil. Composted manure is sold cheaply in bags at the kind of instant garden shops that spring up at discount stores and drugstores each March. Use the amount recommended on the package. Just spread it on and hoe it in lightly, being careful not to cut into roots. Cow or horse manure straight from farm or stable is even better, but put it in your compost pile instead of applying it directly to the garden, because the high nitrogen in fresh manure can burn plants.

Keeping Your Soil Fixed

It's important to recognize that once you fix soil, your job will not be done. You need to maintain nutrients, texture, and moisture-retentive qualities. The plants in your garden will actually use up the organic matter you put into your soil. You don't put a plate of food in front of your family and expect to be done cooking forever. Once the food is consumed you have to provide more. It's the same with a garden. Once the organic matter, bonemeal, and manure are used up you have to provide more. If you have noticed your garden is not doing as well as it once did, you may be neglecting your soil.

Put down compost each fall. Dig in composted manure, compost, and bonemeal whenever you plant, hoe in composted manure in the spring. It sounds like an enormous amount of work, but you probably need the exercise anyway, and done a little at a time it's not that big a burden. You're going to be digging a hole anyway. You might as well make that small extra effort to enrich the soil you've turned.

Compost, bonemeal, composted manure, and gypsum are the four things I load into my wheelbarrow every time I head into the garden. These ingredients add up to my recipe for rich, moist, loamy soil that is nirvana to perennials.

4

Planting and Transplanting

When you choose a plant for your garden, start by checking its winter hardiness for your climate zone. Consult the USDA Plant Hardiness Zone Map in the front of this book (or on the back cover) and select only plants that have a hardiness rating no higher than the zone where you live (further detail on climate zones and hardiness is provided in chapter 1).

Next, consider the heat of summer. Read catalog descriptions carefully and supplement them by consulting garden books that give site information for perennial plants. If catalogs and books say the plant requires full sun with some protection from afternoon sun, you may be dealing with a euphemism that really means Midwestern heat will cook this baby. For Midwestern gardeners, "plant in full sun" is the biggest lie in garden literature. Consider the source. Does the author live in one of those sissy places like England or the Pacific Northwest? Full sun in the Midwest, combined with wind, is a blast furnace that only the toughest will survive. Full sun is good siting for *Hemerocallis* (daylily), irises, roses, *Achillea* (yarrow), asters, chrysanthemums, herbs, and *Lilium lancifolium,* syn. *L. tigrinum*

(tiger lily). If you plan to put *Digitalis* (foxglove), *Astilbe* (false spirea), and *Campanula* (bellflower) in the full sun of our region, however, you might just as well stick them in the oven and be done with it. Even with shade protection, some plants that are theoretically appropriate for our region based on their hardiness rating simply will never be vigorous survivors here. Sometimes heeding the advice of a veteran Midwestern gardener is your best bet for success.

Starting Plants from Seed

You can buy the plant you want locally, order it from a nursery catalog, or start it from seed. The general assumption is that starting seed indoors will save you great buckets of money. After many years of tending flats of seedlings, I don't believe this is true. You'll need equipment and supplies that run into serious money: grow lights, seed flats, seed trays, seed starting mix, plastic sheeting to preserve moisture, plant stakes, and expensive seed packets. After all this expense, you'll still have the occasional crop failure that results in a trip to the nursery to buy the plants, too!

Is it worth the fuss and expense? That depends. If all you want is a few annuals easily purchased locally, then you're wasting time and money growing your own. Likewise, if you want two or three perennials, you're probably money ahead to buy the plants. However, there are times when it makes sense to start seed indoors. For design reasons, you may want several annuals of a specific color instead of the ubiquitous mixed colors sold in nurseries. Or you might want to try something new that can't be had except in seed form. Or you might want to plant masses of a particular perennial and don't want to fork over the price for two dozen pots of it. These are all good reasons to start the seeds yourself indoors. There's one more good reason. Tending a few trays of seeds is a great way to counteract the cabin fever of February.

Check each packet to find out when to plant seeds. If the packet suggests starting zinnias six weeks before planting, just count six weeks back from the frost-free date and mark your calendar. It doesn't pay to get in a rush and start seeds early. They will grow large too soon and become leggy from inadequate sunlight. In zone 5, the frost-free date occurs sometime in mid-May; in zone 4, it's later. Ask an experienced gardener or the local nursery staff for the specific date where you live.

If you have a south-facing window, you might just get away with growing a few seedlings without artificial light, but most likely you'll need to invest in light fixtures and special grow light bulbs. Check the nursery or hardware store. Install the lights so they can be adjusted up and down. It's a good idea to get a timer, too, so that lights can be set to go on and off automatically.

Fill your seed flats with a seed starting mix. It will be lightweight, for easy penetration by tiny roots, and moisture retentive. Check the package before you buy to be sure the mix contains some milled sphagnum peat moss to prevent an outbreak of damping off. This fungal disease attacks small seedlings and fells them within hours. The price of a seed starting mix is well worth it to avoid this guilt-producing disaster.

The soil should be moist but not dripping. The easiest way to achieve this is to put water directly into the bag and give the potting mix time to soak it up before you plant. Warm water will soak in faster. If you're in a rush, dump the soil mix into a wheelbarrow, add water, and mix with your gloved hands. Fill the seed flats and allow any excess water to drain off for about thirty minutes.

You can plant seeds in rows or broadcast them over the entire surface of the containers. Cover the seeds with soil or leave them exposed, according to packet instructions. Some seeds require light to germinate and some require darkness, so it's important to check the package. Don't forget to label the seeds. I like to write the planting date and number of days needed for germination right on the plant stake. Later, when the seeds haven't sprouted yet, I can check to see if they're overdue.

Line up your containers under lights and set the lights about three inches above the soil surface. Drape plastic sheeting or kitchen plastic wrap over the trays to retain moisture. You can put a few plastic stakes around the edge of the flat to hold the plastic above the soil. Run the lights about twelve hours a day. When the seeds sprout, remove the plastic. As the seedlings grow, raise the lights to keep them about three to six inches above the plant tops.

Watch the flats closely for drying. When the surface of the seed starter mix looks pale, it needs water. To avoid toppling tiny seedlings, water from the bottom. Put water in the plastic trays and set the seed flats into them. After half an hour dump out any excess water. Once the plants have developed a couple of sets of true leaves, you can water them from above using a gentle spray. I'm speaking here of true leaves, not the rounded cotyledons that first emerge from the seed (cotyledons are the food storage units within the seed that allow a plant to get going before it puts out true leaves to begin photosynthesis).

As the plants grow, thin them to prevent crowding. Remove excess seedlings to leave the remaining ones an inch or two apart. Use your fingers or snip them off with a pair of manicure scissors. Snipping is quicker and prevents damage to the roots of the plants that remain.

Experts usually recommend that you move the seedlings once they have one or two sets of true leaves and pot them individually. This may be ideal, but it is time-consuming. You can skip this step by simply planting directly from the seed flat into the garden. Alternatively, you can plant into small pots in the first place or use the six-packs in which you buy annuals. Plant just two or three seeds in each container and thin them to one plant when it's clear which seedling is strongest. Set the six-packs into a seed flat and put the flat into a tray to make bottom watering easy. Simply lift out the whole flat of six-packs when you're finished watering.

Not every seed you plant will germinate, and some kinds of seed will sprout more completely than others. Seed does best if it's planted fresh. Saving the remains of a partially used packet of seed for a later year can be a disappointing exercise since the old seed may germinate poorly, if at all.

Before setting plants out in the garden, harden them off—in other words, toughen them up a bit. A few days before planting, haul the seed flats outdoors and set them in a protected place where they will get the morning sun, but no direct afternoon sun. A position in dappled shade for the afternoon would do. This accustoms the small plants to stronger light. They will dry out rapidly outdoors, especially if it's windy, so check them a couple of times a day and water as needed. Watch the temperature carefully and run the seedlings back indoors if it looks like temperatures will drop anywhere near freezing. Don't leave seedlings out in the rain because the drops will batter them down and wash the light soil off their roots.

Some plants resent transplanting so strongly that they are best started from seed directly in the garden. *Ocimum basilicum* (basil), *Borago officinalis* (borage), *Lychnis coronaria* (rose campion), *Cleome* (spider flower), and *Consolida* (larkspur) are examples. Others, like early *Tagetes* (marigold) and *Lobularia maritima,* syn. *Alyssum maritimum* (sweet alyssum), shoot up and begin blooming so quickly that starting seed indoors is unnecessary and buying plants is something of an extravagance. If you plant seeds directly into the garden, just follow the instructions printed on the packet. Plant late enough so that the seeds will not germinate before the frost-free date. The larger the seed, the heavier the covering of soil you will put over it. Very fine seeds and those that require light to germinate will not be covered at all. Keep the seed bed moist until germination, then continue to water often until seedlings have at least a couple of pairs of true leaves. Check your seedlings twice a day to be sure they are adequately moist. As they grow more leaves and larger root systems they can withstand more heat and sun. Gradually reduce the amount of water.

Purchasing from a Local Nursery

If you decide to bypass the seed-starting process and purchase plants instead, it's usually best to buy from a local nursery, if possible. When compared to mail-ordered plants, local purchases are likely to be healthier, larger, and less expensive. They haven't been stressed by being wrapped and shut in a box for several days. You have a chance to examine them before buying to assess size and vigor. You don't have to pay the often exorbitant shipping and handling charges. Local nursery staff can advise you and answer questions. Plants found for sale locally are more likely to be suitable to our climate. Add to all these reasons the pleasure of being able to support a local business and your own community and you have ample reason to purchase plants at home.

Be cautious about buying plants locally, however, at places other than established nurseries. The plants available at drugstores, lumberyards, grocery stores, and the other plants stands that pop up in spring are usually shipped from distant nurseries while they're in good condition, but may not receive proper care once they arrive at their destination. Unless you buy the plants on the day they were unloaded from the truck, they're probably going to be stressed.

Serious garden planning gets going in January, right after the frenzy of the holidays. This is when you have the time and peace to consider the coming garden season. Make yourself a pot of tea, sit down, and dream. Once you've made a list of the plants you want to acquire, decide whether to mail order or buy locally. If you have haunted local nurseries in previous years, you already have a good idea whether a specific plant is going to be available. When in doubt, phone the nursery. By midwinter staff there should know what will be in stock come spring.

Ordering by Mail

While there are many reasons to buy locally, there is only one to order by mail: the plant you want isn't offered for sale in your area. When you must order by mail, go slowly. Don't assume that a high price guarantees a fine specimen. For similar prices, you may purchase a daylily from two different mail order nurseries and receive drastically different plants. The roots of one may be the size of half your fist while the other has hardly a tablespoon of root structure. An inflated price may suggest that a plant is exotic or rare, but the very same plant may be available elsewhere for half as much.

One reason prices can be so outrageous is that catalog production is costly. If the catalog before you features page upon page of beautiful color photographs, the price of plants will reflect the cost of its production. If the company does considerable national advertising, that cost, too, will be passed along to you. On the other hand, the big, flashy catalogs represent firms that are long established and likely to stand behind their products. A catalog without illustration is far less enticing, but the prices may be lower, the plants larger, or very possibly both. For my money, careful descriptions of hardiness, mature size, and site and soil needs are worth more than beautiful photographs. Be extremely wary of catalogs that do not include Latin plant names or hardiness zones. To locate a good source for mail-ordered plants, seek advice from gardening friends.

If you plan to order plants like irises and daylilies that are constantly being crossed to create new cultivars, keep in mind that very high prices are often charged for the latest one. While it is different from earlier and cheaper varieties, it isn't necessarily any better—just newer.

Read plant descriptions with care, trolling for nuance. Words like *spreading* and *vigorous* are often used as nursery euphemisms for "relentlessly invasive." *Centaurea montana* (perennial cornflower or mountain bluet), for example, is characterized as "spreading freely" by one catalog in my possession, when the truth is that this hoodlum expands its territory explosively. If you plant it be prepared to jump back.

Talk to other gardeners about their experience with various mail order houses, then test out several sources by ordering just a few plants from each. You can assess plant size and vigor, packaging, speed of delivery, cost, and viability once the plant is in the ground. That way when you're ready to place a big order you can do so with confidence.

Site Selection: Light and Moisture

Siting plants well is key to their success. Start by finding out whether your latest acquisition requires sun, shade, or something in between. If a plant is suggested for "full sun or sun with some afternoon protection," in our climate full sun will probably be too much for it. Assume that the more protective condition applies. Find a spot that receives direct sun only in the morning. Very light shade all day would suit or morning sun and afternoon shade or morning sun and dappled afternoon light. Our sun is extremely hot and direct between about 1:00 and 4:00 P.M. during the summer. At this crucial time of day many perennials require some respite.

For plants requiring shade, remember that not all shade is the same. Under closely planted trees the shade is dense. A single tree casts moderate shade. A shrub or fence may create a temporary area of light shade. The denser the shade the easier it will be to keep the soil moist. Dense shade with numerous tree roots, however, dries out the ground quickly. Some shade plants will not tolerate dense shade. Pay attention to the nuance of description in catalogs and books and plant accordingly, always remembering that sun and part sun are hotter and less hospitable in our area than in other parts of the country that share our hardiness zone. When in doubt, go a degree shadier.

Before you put shovel to dirt, you'll also need to know what a plant wants in the way of moisture. A moisture-retentive soil is great for *Astilbe* (false spirea), Siberian irises, and *Anemone*, but certain death for tall bearded irises. You may notice that certain spots in your garden remain wet longer following a rain. In these poor drainage areas, you must either thoroughly amend the soil to improve drainage or plant only what likes wet feet, such as *Astilbe* or *Iris pseudacorous* (yellow flag).

Locate plants with similar moisture requirements together. It's much easier to water a whole bed with a sprinkler or soaker hose than to water each plant individually according to its own needs.

Allow for Mature Size

At planting time, keep in mind how slowly many perennials grow. Those in small containers (two or three inches across) are probably grown from seed and only a few weeks old. They can't be expected to reach a mature size or to bloom much in their first season or even their second. Plants in containers of quart size or larger, on the other hand, are already a year old and will perform far more quickly. In a hurry to have a show? Buy bigger plants. Want to save money? Buy smaller ones and give them time to mature.

You should, from the beginning, allow the full space your perennial will demand when mature, especially for difficult to move plants like *Hosta* (hosta or plantain lily), *Baptisia australis* (blue wild indigo, false indigo, or plains false indigo), Siberian irises, roses, and shrubs. These quickly become large, heavy, and tough to transplant. During their immature stage, you can put a ground cover at their feet or surround them with annuals to fill the void. Hostas look especially pretty with pansies crowded in amongst them. Alternatively, smaller, easy-to-move perennials can first be planted into a nursery bed. After a year or two when they are more nearly mature size, you can set them into place in a border. This works fine for those that are still a manageable size at maturity, assuming you have the space for a nursery bed. Unless you have a large property, however, this may be a luxury you can't afford.

When to Plant

Perennials can be planted anytime after the ground thaws in spring, usually about four to six weeks before the frost-free date. Because they become established more easily if weather remains cool for about two weeks after they are planted, early is better than late. If you wait until mid-May or later to put perennials in the ground, they are likely to face heat and hot wind during their critical first two weeks, and extra watering will be required.

Most annuals, on the other hand, require warm nights to really begin growing and will not recover if their tops freeze. Wait to plant them until all danger of frost is past. If you are planting seeds rather than plants, you can probably fudge and sow them a week early, as temperatures do not have to be above freezing until the seeds have sprouted. Once you've reached the frost-free date, waste no time. Get your annuals into the ground pronto. This gives them a good start before the heat of summer hits. If you plant more than two weeks after the frost-free date, daytime temperatures will have climbed high enough to desiccate tender seedlings and small plants.

Three annuals that fare best if planted very early are *Viola* x *wittrockiana* (pansy), *Antirrhinum* (snapdragon), and sweet alyssum. They thrive in cool weather and need it to do really well, putting on a good show in spring, but sulking in summer. Snapdragons and sweet alyssum will bloom well again in the cool of fall, but often pansies have curled up their toes by then. To take advantage of their lovely spring bloom and give them the best possible start, set out plants very early—about two or three weeks before the frost-free date for snapdragons or sweet alyssum and four to six weeks ahead of the frost-free date for pansies.

Digging the Hole

You've chosen the right plant, checked on its likes and dislikes, decided where to put it; now it's time to get down to business. First, dig a hole. Now, dig it bigger. The adage is, for a dime-size plant, dig a dollar-size hole. To give a plant a good start, dig a hole at least a few inches deeper than the plant is—to accommodate the roots— and several inches wider. If the plant has eight inches of roots, you want a hole that is about twelve inches deep and about sixteen inches wide. The extra-big hole allows you to put loose dirt all the way around and below the root structure, giving roots an easy start. For a shrub or tree, dig the hole extra wide, but only as deep as necessary to accommodate the roots. This allows for plenty of surrounding loose dirt, but prevents the heavy plant from sinking into soft dirt below it.

Now is the time to improve the soil. You've already done the hard work of digging the dirt out of the hole. Take a few extra minutes to improve it. Dig in gypsum if you're working with clay. Add compost, bonemeal, and, if your plant likes a rich soil, add a bit of composted manure. Mix it all up with your shovel and toss some of this beautiful stuff into the bottom of the hole. Next, set the plant in place and fill in all around it with the loose soil you've made. Water the plant in to be sure there are no air pockets left around roots and to give it the moisture it will need to help it survive the shock of transplanting. If you have more soil than you need, use the excess to form a ring around the plant a few inches out from the stem. This will capture water when it rains or when you irrigate. The ring will gradually melt down into the surrounding soil, but meanwhile it helps your plant obtain plenty of moisture while it's getting established.

Transplanting

As you refine your garden design and increase plant stock by dividing, you will do lots of transplanting. Make careful notes while your garden is in bloom about changes you plan to make. Daylilies have a vast range of bloom color, size, and form, but once they stop flowering, their identical foliage makes them indistinguishable. The same is true of irises. You might want to mark plants to be moved with a stake. It's easiest to decide what to move when you can see what is already in flower where you intend to put something new. Pick a leaf and blossom from the plant you want to move and compare them to leaf and blossom of neighbors where you will place it. It's surprising how often a combination imagined in your head is far less attractive when you put the articles in question side by side. Be reasonable in what you plan, because it takes longer to move things with a shovel than it does with your imagination. Unless you have a big, burly, and compliant assistant, you may find you've bitten off more than you can chew.

Time transplanting carefully. Plants are best moved during cool weather after bloom. For spring-blooming plants wait until the cool of fall, probably sometime in September, to transplant. For fall bloomers transplant in the cool of spring. Summer bloomers can be moved in either spring or fall. Foliage plants are best transplanted in spring, when they can be dug and divided before the leaves unfold, minimizing damage. Hostas, for instance, are best moved in spring, when their leaves are newly emerged but still tightly furled in points.

Spring transplanting can be done in the month before the frost-free date—as soon as the ground is warm, workable, and no longer sticky wet from frost and snow. If you transplant in autumn, plants should ideally have six weeks to get over the shock of being moved before freezing temperatures begin. Determine the date of likely first frost and try to do your transplanting six weeks ahead of it.

Having stated the rules, let me add that you probably can manage, if you absolutely must, to transplant most plants even during the heat of summer. Water very frequently until the plant becomes established and provide some shade, especially in the afternoon. Shade can be cast by an overturned box or bushel basket or the woven seat of a lawn chair. It takes a lot of fiddling and personal attention, but it can be done.

Most transplanting is done because you're refining your garden design, but another very good reason to transplant is to increase stock of a desired perennial. With a great many perennials this is surprisingly easy to do. It's just a question of digging up the plant and then literally dividing it into whatever number of plants you need. As violent as it sounds, you can do this by simply plunging your shovel right through, slicing both foliage and roots. With some vigorous growers, like chrysanthemums, asters, and irises, it's best to hack off and replant the outer pieces of new growth, discarding the inner, older parts. Quite small divisions will grow. A *Nepeta* (catmint) plant one foot across could be cut into nine four-inch-square pieces, each of which would make a full-size plant by the end of the second season. The slower growing the plant, the larger the pieces should be if you want a reasonable show quickly.

When you move a plant, do the job in a hurry. Dig a nice big hole and prepare the soil first. Then—and only then—dig the plant to be moved. To decrease root damage, be sure to leave a nice amount of dirt attached to the roots. Put the plant immediately into the hole you've prepared, fill dirt in around the roots, and water well at once. By moving a plant in this way, you can trick it into thinking it's never been moved at all. If for some reason the plant has been dug and a place is not yet prepared, be sure to keep the plant in a shady spot.

Patience

There's an old saying about perennials: The first year they sleep, the second year they creep, the third year they leap. This is an axiom I wish I had heard as a young gardener when I was impatient, booting a plant out if it failed to perform by the end of its first season. Judging a perennial before its third year is like writing a book review without reading beyond the first fifty pages.

I planted a *Filipendula purpurea* (Japanese meadowsweet) that made a mere scrap of a plant its first year, hardly lifting its leaves a foot above ground. The second year it was knee-high and bloomed beautifully, filling its allotted space and displaying lovely pale green maplelike leaves. *Aquilegia canadensis* 'Corbett' (Canada columbine), a dainty pale yellow columbine that looked wildly enticing in a mail order catalog, didn't bloom at all in its first year. The second year it was so loaded with bloom that even my nongardening, color-blind husband commented.

Some plants take more than three years to achieve their full splendor. *Hosta sieboldiana* var. *elegans,* for example, won't reach its colossal shrublike size for six or seven years. I planted two in my shade border and was disappointed with their paltry size after three years. When one of them had to be moved two years later, it required the efforts of two strong men to accomplish the project. *Baptisia australis* (blue wild indigo, false indigo, or plains false indigo), many clematis, and *Polygonatum odoratum* 'Variegatum' (fragrant Solomon's seal) are other examples of slow starters. Conversely, some perennials reach a perfectly respectable size in just two years. There is no hard and fast rule, in spite of the tidy little rhyme quoted above. The point is to have patience. Put your plant in the ground and give it time to reach its full glory.

5

Favorites Flowers for the Hot Midwest . . . & a Few Troublemakers

This is an unabashedly personal catalog of favorite garden plants, not an all-inclusive listing of winter-hardy plants for our region. Most of these have become favorites after years of trial and error for solid reasons—beauty of both flower and foliage, long bloom seasons, the oomph to stand up to heat and humidity, sturdy health, glorious color. I love them and I have my reasons. The plants listed here are suitable for both the cold winters *and* the hot summers in our area. These are four-star beauties for your Midwestern paradise.

Difficult Plants for the Hot and Cold Midwest

Not all plants that are theoretically winter hardy in our area will survive severe cold without snow cover or thrive in our scorching heat. Although they are listed as hardy in zones 4 and 5, I specifically warn you against the plants listed below. You may have good luck with them in a mild year or so-so results through year after year of typical weather, but don't expect robust performance over the long haul, particularly if you have heavy clay soil:

Antirrhinum (snapdragon)—except cultivars labeled heat toler-
   ant, like Liberty Series
Calendula officinalis (pot marigold)
Campanula (bellflower)
Centranthus ruber (red valerian)
Clarkia, syn. *Godetia*
Delphinium
Digitalis (foxglove)
Iberis sempervirens (candytuft)
Lavandula (lavender)
Linum (flax)
Lobelia—annual
Matthiola (stock)
Monarda (bee balm or bergamot)—cultivars not labeled disease
   resistant
Phlox paniculata (garden phlox)—cultivars not labeled disease
   resistant
Platycodon grandiflorus (balloon flower)
Primula (primrose)
Veronica (speedwell)—except the creepers

In spite of this warning, I have included two of these troublemak-
ers among my favorites: delphiniums and foxgloves. These two are
so ravishingly irresistible in spite of their shortcomings that I
couldn't leave them out. Although I do not recommend them, some
gardeners find them worth the bother and risk when they manage
to survive both summer and winter.

Favorites

To make garden planning easy, I've listed the plants chronologically in order of bloom, beginning with the earliest. Since plants have
varying and overlapping bloom periods, they are placed in the list
according to date they first begin to bloom, but some long bloomers
are placed according to their most significant bloom time. These

times offer a general guideline only, because weather variations from year to year and your garden's microclimate will cause vagaries in precise dates and length of bloom. Early spring bloomers and the last flowers of fall are especially affected. The specific bloom times mentioned are primarily for zone 5. If you live in zone 4, bloom times are likely to be a couple of weeks later. Bloom time is so important in garden design that you can't start too soon keeping a notebook in which you record weekly what is in bloom in your garden. Chapter 8 presents a sequence of bloom times for these and many more plants to help you in garden planning.

Spring Bulbs

Much of the first wave of spring bloom—some of it actually occurring before winter ends—is made up of bulbs. Because these clever plants form their spring foliage and flower a year ahead, storing them away underground, they are particularly reliable bloomers. They bring the colors we so desperately need after the drab landscape of winter. They can, however, be very tricky to place in a garden design for three reasons. First, their foliage must be left to ripen and brown before it is removed so that next year's flower will form. Second, the dormancy that follows bloom and ripening will, in the case of bulbs planted in groupings, create big empty places in your garden. Third, once dormant, the bulbs' locations become vague in your mind, leading to nasty bulb-jabbing accidents when you start putting your shovel in where it doesn't belong.

The smaller the bulb foliage, the more quickly it will ripen and cease to be unsightly in your garden. Early bulbs like *Galanthus nivalis* (common snowdrop), crocuses, *Puschkinia scilloides* (striped squill), and *Chionodoxa luciliae*, syn. *C. gigantea* (glory of the snow) ripen their small, grassy leaves rapidly. Tulips and particularly daffodils, however, have large leaves that ripen slowly, creating quite a mess in the garden. After years of planting tulip bulbs, I have finally realized that the best way to cope with their postbloom foliage is to plant them in singles or small groupings. A clump of ten or twelve tulips makes quite a patch of ugly brown foliage at a certain stage, unless you can creatively disguise it with growing perennials, groundcover, or annuals. I prefer smaller plantings of one, three, or five tulips, which are far less noticeable when the foliage browns. Fortuitously, this approach also creates a prettier garden. Let's say you have a fifty-foot garden and thirty bulbs to plant. If you plant two clumps of fifteen bulbs, you have two big, widely separated splotches of color. On the other hand, by spacing out three single bulbs, four groupings of three bulbs, and three groupings of five, you can give the impression of bloom throughout the bed. This alone, regardless of what else is in flower, will give your garden a feeling of unity, assuming you stick with some color scheme.

Daffodil foliage is your worst nightmare—lots of leaves that take a long time ripening. Occasionally you will see a garden in which someone has braided the foliage after the bloom ceased. This may interfere with proper ripening of the leaves and thus with flower formation, although I haven't tested the theory myself since I think braided daffodils look idiotic. A better solution is to disguise the foliage with that of surrounding plants.

If you choose to plant tulips and daffodils in clumps, they will leave a considerable empty spot following removal of browned foliage unless you have laid your plans in advance. You can fill the space with annuals. If the bulbs are early bloomers, you'll be able to plant seeds or put annuals right into the vacancy. Later blooming bulbs ripen so late that it will be too hot for seedlings. Try potting up a few annuals and growing them on your patio until they are needed to disguise bulb gaps. Then just tap them out of their pots and plant them without disturbing their roots. Obviously, this method works only with large bulbs, which are planted deep. With shallow bulb plantings, try putting the annuals directly behind the bulbs.

Another way to fill the space is to plant bulbs among bushy perennials that spread out as the season progresses. They need relatively little space while the bulbs are in bloom but will fill in as the bulbs go dormant. This works well with daylilies, asters, and chrysanthemums. You might also try it with *Calamintha* (calamint), *Nepeta* (catmint), *Gypsophila paniculata* (baby's breath), *Buddleia davidii* (butterfly bush), and *Perovskia atriplicifolia* (Russian sage).

Make careful note of exactly where bulbs are planted so that during their dormancy you don't mistakenly plunge a shovel in amongst them. I confess that in spite of garden charts, plant labels, and memories of last spring, I am myself a wanton bulb slicer. I have finally, though, learned to be philosophical about an occasional loss. Once you have whacked a piece off a bulb, discard it and get on with your life.

Galanthus nivalis (common snowdrop), bulb, height four–six inches, spread two–three inches, shade or part shade: A friend who has a breathtaking woodland wildflower garden tells me that snowdrops must always be planted in groups, as they are sociable and do best in company. It's a nice conceit, but in any case they are so small that if you want to make a show, you must follow her advice and plant them in numbers. The delicate, pendant white blooms are the first to appear in my garden, starting near the end of February and lasting about three weeks. Microclimates have a strong influence on these very early bulbs. The aforementioned friend lives less than a mile from my garden and her snowdrops bloom the first of February, nearly a month ahead of mine. It is not at all unusual to experience a snowfall during the snowdrops' bloom, and they appear so charming and gallant blooming with snow at their feet that photographs of them in this situation are almost a cliché of garden literature. Plant them about three inches deep and three inches apart in shade or part shade. They like rich soil with plenty of humus added. Snowdrops will return year after year with no additional care, and if happy will spread themselves from seed.

Crocus, bulb, height four inches, spread one–three inches, sun: In my mother's garden crocuses were the first flowers to bloom each spring, so for me they have a special magic. I've long thought their fat pastel blooms look like the broken shells of Easter eggs. Though all the plants in this large genus of bulbs are no taller than snowdrops, most display disproportionately large blooms, which render them much flashier. *Crocus ancyrensis* (golden bunch crocus), however, is a very early and tiny bright yellow one that always blooms for me at the end of February or early in March. Its bloom is so small that it creates no show at all unless you plant several, but it does weather late spring storms better than the larger crocuses that bloom two weeks later. Crocuses come primarily in white, yellow, and purple shades. I especially admire a wonderful lavender-and-white-striped version: *C. vernus* 'Pickwick' (Dutch crocus). I plant these at the front of my border with perennials behind them that will grow up and spill over the space the crocuses leave behind as they die back. Plant all crocuses three inches deep in a sunny spot or in the shade of deciduous trees (those which drop their leaves each fall). The crocuses will go dormant before the trees cloak themselves in leaves.

Narcissus (daffodil), bulb, size varies, sun: This large genus has about fifty species and hundreds of cultivars split into twelve groups based primarily on flower shape. In a good year, daffodils bloom over a period of several weeks—the very embodiment of springtime in their liquid sunshine yellows and frosty whites. Their fragrance is heavenly sweet and their blossoms, nodding in the spring breeze, seem perpetually filled with sunlight. In a bad year they will be battered to the ground by driving rains, their sod-

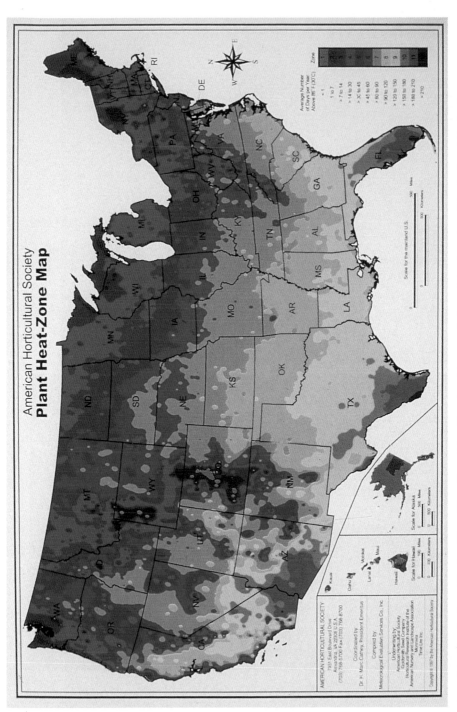

American Horticultural Society Plant Heat-Zone Map (Reprinted by permission of the American Horticultural Society).

Nicotiana sylvestris (garden of Catherine Angle and John Angle).

Sunny border combining various plant shapes and heights to create a pleasing design: *Thymus* (thyme), *Dianthus deltoides* 'Brilliant' (pink), tall bearded *Iris,* and *Lilium* (lily).

Tulipa 'Heart's Delight' with *Narcissus* 'February Gold' (daffodil).

Mixed *Hemerocallis* (daylilies; garden of Aileen Rodgers and Jack Rodgers; photo by Jack Rodgers).

Hosta 'Undulata Albomarginata' (hosta or plantain lily) with *Aquilegia canadensis* (Canada columbine) and *Phlox divaricata* (woodland phlox or wild sweet William).

Right: Hosta 'Krossa Regal' (hosta or plantain lily), *Athyrium niponicum* (Japanese painted fern), *Cystopteris fragilis* (fragile fern), *Hosta* 'Frances Williams.'

Below: *Veronica* 'Waterperry' (speedwell) at front. *Geranium* 'Johnson's Blue' at back.

Below: Hosta 'Undulata Albomarginata' (hosta or plantain lily) with foliage of *Astilbe* 'Brautschleier,' syn. *A.* 'Bridal Veil' (false spirea) and *Aquilegia canadensis* (Canada columbine).

den blossoms splattered with mud. The early heat (which comes so often to our part of the country that you have to wonder why we call it unseasonably hot weather) will be accompanied by a blast furnace wind that dries the flowers to a crisp in less than a day. Then there's that endless period while you wait for the foliage to feed the bulb for next year's bloom and *go away.* For several weeks—certainly much longer than the bloom lasted—you must put up with disreputable foliage that flops over, shrivels, and turns yellow. When finally it is brown enough that you can pull it up and compost it, you are left—if you have planted your daffodils in clumps—with great gaping holes in your garden that must be dealt with craftily.

Why would you put up with all this? Simply because daffodils in a good year are stunningly beautiful. They light up the garden and lift the heart. Even in a bad year, you can cut them to enjoy indoors while the rains and winds blast away outside. Furthermore, these bulbs bloom reliably year after year. Plant a tulip and you will most likely enjoy really fine bloom only once. Plant a daffodil and you will watch it bloom and increase for many years to come. (The daffodils planted in the early 1800s by William Wordsworth and his sister, Dorothy, at Rydal Mount, their home in the English Lake District, still bloom each spring.) In addition, unlike many of the bulbs you spend your limited garden budget on, these create large and showy flowers. They are undoubtedly an excellent investment when it comes to beauty and longevity.

We live in a region where heavy snow in April is by no means unheard of, but also where temperatures can reach the nineties in the same season—even in the same year! It seems to me, however, that heat and wind are more the rule when daffodils bloom. For this reason, I think the Midwestern gardener does better to emphasize daffodils that bloom early or midseason and forgo the later-blooming ones. The earlier they put on their show, the less likely they are to be blasted by the hot winds that absolutely ruin them. Fortunately, snow doesn't seem to faze them in the least, as long as temperatures don't plummet. Early bloomers have the added advantage of ripening their foliage and stepping aside earlier.

I have a few favorites among this large group of flowers. *Narcissus* 'Tête-à-Tête' is a miniature daffodil, commonly available in pots at your florist or nursery or even grocery store in winter. Buy a pot to enjoy indoors in February—that dreary month that can scarcely be borne without forced bulbs and cut flowers in the house. After the bloom, keep watering until the foliage has turned brown. By then spring is well begun and you can find a spot in the garden to plant the bulbs five inches deep and four-five inches apart. Unlike many forced bulbs, they will bloom in the garden very nicely the following spring. Just six inches tall, with small golden yellow blooms that begin about mid-March and last about two weeks, they are a treasure indoors and out. *N.* 'February Gold' is an early bloomer that is small (ten–twelve inches tall) but very sturdy. Its flowers, beginning about mid-April, are pure, beautiful yellow. The foliage seems to ripen very rapidly, making far less untidiness than larger daffodils.

N. 'Thalia' never fails to delight garden visitors. Its unusual ivory white blooms, very faintly yellow when first open, four to five to a twelve-inch stem, look like clusters of orchids, very pleasing and elegant. A midseason bloomer, 'Thalia' seems less affected by hot winds than other daffodils. Both 'Thalia' and 'February Gold' are extremely reliable, coming back year after year. Another good return bloomer is 'Carlton,' with a two-toned yellow bloom.

Plant daffodils in full sunlight or light dappled shade, but remember that those with pink or red cups retain their color best if they are given a bit of shade. Depth of planting varies with the size of the bulb, so follow the supplier's instructions. Site daffodils carefully; they are not easy to move and can stay a very long time in one location. If you must transplant them, dig the hole you will put them in first. They don't appreciate being left out of the ground to dry up, so make the move as quickly as possible, being very careful not to leave the exposed bulbs in the sun. Transplanting is best accomplished just as the foliage finishes drying and when the bulbs are dormant, but still easy to find.

Plan ahead to fill the space left behind when daffodils have finished their show. I have a large number of daffodils planted in my herb garden in small patches (about eighteen to twenty-four inches across) between the herbs. As the daffodil foliage emerges from the ground, I cut back the previous year's growth on most of the herbs to a few inches from the ground. After the daffodils have departed, the spreading foliage of *Thymus* (thyme), *Origanum* (oregano), *Salvia officinalis* (common sage), *Allium schoenoprasum* (chives), and *Mentha* (mint) fills the allotted space. In my sunny border, daffodils are planted among daylilies, whose similar straplike foliage helps to disguise the fading leaves of the bulbs. By the time the daffodils finish, the daylilies have increased in size and nicely fill the gaps.

Chionodoxa luciliae, syn. *C. gigantea* (glory of the snow), bulb, height four–five inches, sun: *Chionodoxa luciliae* is a lovely little bulb, less frequently seen in gardens than the similar *Scilla siberica* (Siberian squill). Both have piercingly sapphire blue blooms only about a half inch across. They grow well in sun or in the shade of deciduous trees. Both can be naturalized in grass, where they will ripen their foliage before the first mowing. Both bloom early in April and will spread from seed. A handful will eventually turn into a sheet of blue. From a distance you might easily mistake the one for the other, but the blossom of the Siberian squill is pendant while glory of the snow faces upward and shows a splotch of white at its center. This difference in coloration and orientation makes glory of the snow showier and, I think, a better choice.

Tulipa (tulip), bulb, size varies, sun: This large genus has about a hundred species and hundreds more cultivars separated into fifteen divisions based primarily on flower shape. Thanks to this huge variety, the tulip season runs from about the middle of March until the last of May, starting with the species tulips. If you want tulips throughout that six-week season, plant several different kinds, paying attention to the supplier's comments on bloom time (very early, early, midseason, and so on). Some suppliers offer mixed tulips that give a good span of bloom and may even be available by color scheme.

In general, tulips bloom best in their first year only. Darwin hybrids are said to be the most reliable for return bloom. The small species tulips are second best. Others lose much of their vigor after the first year, with blooms reduced in both size and number. By their third or fourth year, and often by their second, tulips send up leaves, but cease to flower. For this reason, I treat them like annuals and plant new bulbs each fall. This may seem an extravagance, but at an average of fifty cents per bulb, I can make a very nice display for not a large investment. When spring rolls around and I have weeks of overlapping waves of bloom, I never begrudge my fall expenditure.

Tulips are supposed to be planted in full sun. Since deciduous trees may not leaf out until tulips have finished blooming, this leaves some latitude. The flowers finish and the foliage can get some sunshine before the trees leaf out so heavily that they shade the bulbs out. You can plant tulips even in the shade of evergreens if you count on just one season of bloom. The blossom is already in the bulb when you buy it, so the first year of bloom is unaffected by a shady site.

The choice of tulips is very wide, so make your selection based on the colors and shapes you prefer and the bloom time you want. I find the small species tulips especially appealing for their early bloom, their diminutive size, and their indefinable sweetness. *Tulipa* 'Heart's Delight' (Kaufmanniana Group) is a special favorite, with its ruffled leaves faintly striped purplish brown and its dark pink bloom with lighter pink edge and yellow interior base. A wonderful species tulip is *T. clusiana* 'Cynthia' with spindly bluish foliage and narrow blooms that alternate petals of pale yellow and a faded coral red. It clashes—just—with the pink of *Dicentra spectabilis* (bleeding heart) but looks terrific with the purple-bronze leaf of *Heuchera micrantha* var. *diversifolia* 'Palace Purple.' *T. clusiana* blooms in mid-May. Among the late bloomers, I think the lily-flowered tulips are standouts. Their large, flared, and pointed petals and their stately height give them great elegance. As with other tulips, the size of the blossom actually grows after it is fully open (even as a cut flower). At its peak of bloom, the flower can be enormous. The lily-flowered tulips last a long time in the garden and also make lovely and long-lasting cut flowers. I enjoy *T.* 'Ballade' (medium purple, edged with white) and *T.* 'Mariette' (rose). If you like a rich yellow, try *T.* 'West Point.'

Muscari (grape hyacinth), bulb, height eight inches, sun: Grape hyacinths have an unusually long bloom season for spring bulbs. From mid-April until late May they create a wave of color. Most are vivid blue. Each kind (there are about thirty species plus cultivars) blooms about four weeks. They seem unaffected by driving rain, howling wind, or early heat. The dense, cone-shaped clusters of little bells make enchanting bouquets if you can bear to cut short their bloom in your garden.

Let's be honest, though. There is a drawback—their summer-dormant foliage. Shortly after bloom, their fat leaves and stems die back and the bulb remains dormant until late in the summer when it suddenly puts on fresh new foliage for the last few weeks of the growing season. The difficulty, of course, is that you must somehow fill the space left vacant at the height of the growing season, while still leaving the space open again in late summer for the resurgence of foliage. Tricky.

You can plant your grape hyacinths toward the back of the bed and place something in front of them that will grow up to disguise their absence at midsummer, but not so tall as to shade them out in late summer. In one bed, I have grape hyacinths planted at the feet of *Paeonia* (peony) with *Geum triflorum* (prairie smoke) in front of them. The coloring of the blue *Muscari* is appealing in combination with the emerging dark reddish-purple peony leaves behind it and the soft rose of prairie smoke in the foreground. In front of the prairie smoke is a planting of *Calamintha nepeta* (lesser calamint), which grows up to take center stage with its airy bloom by late July, and with its foliage long before then. In another bed, the grape hyacinths are planted near an *Aster* x *frikartii* 'Mönch,' which grows up and then flops over to cover the gap following the grape hyacinths' bloom, but stays low enough to allow the later rebirth of foliage to poke up through it.

Other Early Spring Bloomers

Vinca minor (dwarf periwinkle, myrtle), perennial, height eight inches, spreading habit, sun or shade: This gradually spreading ground cover bears glossy, dark green leaves. It blooms about four weeks—from mid-April through mid-May—with minor, sporadic bloom likely throughout the summer and fall. The flowers are blue with a hint of lavender. *Vinca minor* makes an excellent ground cover around shrubs, under trees, and in confined areas, but does not mix well with perennials or annuals in a border. It may take some time to get established, but grows densely, puts its roots in firmly, and is difficult to remove. It does seem to coexist with bulbs. Just make sure you choose bulbs whose flowers and foliage will be tall enough to stand above the myrtle. It is remarkably adaptable, growing equally well in full sun and dense shade.

Viola x *wittrockiana* (pansy), annual, height eight inches, sun or
shade: The pansy must be one of the sweetest flowers ever to
grace a garden. The "face" among its petals gives it a special appeal for children, which may explain why so many of us are nos-
talgic about them as adults. Another part of its charm is that
cutting it only encourages further bloom. As my mother (who
adores this flower) always says, "If you want pansies, cut pansies."
They are showy planted in groups of six or more. They make
wonderful filler around junior perennials that have a few years
to go before they expand into their allotted space. My most inspired use of them in my own garden was to surround young
variegated *Hosta* (hosta or plantain lily) with blue pansies. As the
hosta leaves unfurled, the pansies wove their way delicately
among them.

For years, I planted pansies too late, thinking they should go in
the ground with other annuals around mid-May. Pansies revel in
cool weather. Buy them the minute you see them for sale and plant
them promptly. They can take temperatures below freezing without collapsing as other annuals will. This early planting—about
four weeks before the frost-free date—will give you a long cool
season of spring bloom, through the end of June. Admittedly the
strong heat of summer that usually hits in July will cause the pansies to dwindle. Bloom will stop and the plants may gasp their last.
Even so, you've already had six weeks of bloom. In a milder summer, planted in shade, your pansies may survive until fall and give
you a bonus few weeks of late season bloom.

Pansies can be planted in light to moderate shade or in sun with
afternoon protection. The sunnier the site, the earlier in summer
they will cease blooming. Pansies have apparently been bred lately
to be more hardy. In recent years, some cultivars have been developed that live through the winter and bloom well the following year, and even ordinary cultivars sometimes make it. The heat

of our region's summers does sap their strength, though, so it's unwise to rely on this trait. If your ordinary pansies survive through summer to bloom in fall, rejoice. If they make it through winter to bloom a second year, consider it a lucky fluke.

Spring

Pulmonaria (lungwort), perennial, height twelve–eighteen inches, spread twenty-four inches, shade: Its leaves softly speckled with silver, *Pulmonaria* is a very desirable, though short-lived, perennial shade plant. Its beauty and the length of its bloom make it a solid contributor. From early or mid-April till the last of May, lungwort puts on a spring show of bloom. The mottled leaves shimmer on throughout the growing season, bringing light to the darkness of shade. As temperatures skyrocket in the hottest part of summer, the leaves may suffer and die back somewhat, so it is best planted among weaving plants such as *Lamium* (deadnettle) or *Galium odoratum,* syn. *Asperula odorata* (sweet woodruff), which can fill in any weakness.

Different types of *Pulmonaria* have white, pink, blue, red, purple, or violet blooms. The clusters of small bell-shaped flowers of many of them are pink in bud, shifting to blue in bloom. The blue blossoms of *P.* 'Roy Davidson,' *P. saccharata,* and others are truly blue and not some shade of purple. Give lungwort plenty of shade to keep it from collapsing in heat. It appreciates the sort of rich, moist soil that most shade plants find attractive. Powdery mildew is likely to be a problem in the warm and humid part of the season. At best these are short-lived perennials in our climate, not ones that you can divide and increase quickly. Still it takes only two or three to make a nice display.

P. saccharata 'Mrs. Moon' has pale sage speckles on its dark green leaves and flowers about a half inch across. Their blue is a sapphire or cornflower shade. My favorite is *P.* 'Roy Davidson,' which has narrower, firmer leaves with a closely mottled surface and flowers of a subtler sky blue. The splotching on its leaves is very pale silvery green for which the coloring of *Lamium maculatum* 'White Nancy' (spotted deadnettle) is a perfect match.

Mertensia pulmonarioides, syn. *M. virginica* (Virginia bluebells), perennial, height twelve twenty inches, spread ten–twelve inches, shade: The most noteworthy drawback of Virginia bluebells might also be seen as an asset. Once the plants have finished blooming and the temperature begins to rise, they go dormant, leaving a gap in the garden. You can turn this habit to good use by planning ahead. I plant Virginia bluebells among my larger hostas. The bluebells come up and bloom nicely from mid-April to mid-May. Meanwhile the hosta foliage progresses from tight little points to gradually unfurling leaves. The bluebells cease blooming and begin to go dormant just as the hosta leaves fill in their vacated space. It's a magical transition.

Virginia bluebells have the same trick of turning from pink in bud to blue in full bloom that many *Pulmonaria* (lungwort) display. The clusters of bell-like blooms are also similar in form, making these two a poor choice for companion planting in your shade border because they are too much alike to be interesting when paired. Most lungworts also offer a longer bloom season, handsomer leaves, and foliage interest for the entire growing season. These considerations make *Pulmonaria* the obvious choice between the two, unless you are trying to provide bloom in a spring gap that will be closed by other plants as the season marches on, in which case *Mertensia pulmonarioides* is your clear choice.

Viola tricolor (Johnny-jump-up), annual, height eight inches, spread two–three inches, sun: Now here's a little article that can charm your socks off. In the first place, these annuals bloom from mid-June all the way through August. Admittedly the early bloom is best and by August it is definitely waning. Still, bloom on each plant is profuse, and the plants go to seed wantonly so that left unchecked they will seem an ocean of bloom on which all of your other plants ride. With the look of tiny purple and yellow pansy flowers on plants just a few inches tall, they give the impression of sweet delicacy. In fact they are tough little nuts. They grow in full sun, undisturbed by heat or dry conditions. In one spot in my garden, they have gone to seed in a brick patio where they bake daily in the sun and receive very little water, but still they bloom in profusion until July. Everyone who visits my garden comments on this captivating effect. When the Johnnys die back I pull them out of the brick to let other self-seeded interlopers come to the fore, chiefly *Thymophylla tenuiloba,* syn. *Dyssodia tenuiloba* (Dahlberg daisy or golden fleece). Next spring the Johnnys are back again from seed.

Epimedium (barrenwort), perennial, height twelve inches, spreading habit, light to dense shade: The tissue-thin, elongated, heart-shaped leaves of all *Epimedium* make them top-notch perennials for shade even before you consider their other strong points. They thrive in moist, rich soil if you have it, but are equally at home in dry shade, weathering drought nicely, thank you. Their delicate appearance belies their essential toughness and reliability. The plants are very solid with leaves that look fresh and pretty all season, making this a handsome ground cover. The pale green color of the leaves offers a nice contrast with other foliage, especially when the oncoming cool weather of fall varies the color with purple. Now add to these qualities a pendulous and dainty little inverted cup and saucer of a flower that blooms for only a couple of weeks in the first half of May, but is so fragile and appealing that you would grow the plant just for the privilege of seeing it annually, and you have an all-star perennial. The flowers of the many species range from white and yellow to pink, red, and purple.

Corydalis lutea, syn. *Pseudofumaria lutea,* perennial, height twelve inches, spread eighteen inches, shade: I was first attracted to *Corydalis lutea* (not hardy in zone 4) by catalog descriptions that promoted it as a long bloomer, but once I began to grow it I realized that its pale and lacy bluish foliage is its real charm. The sulfur yellow flowers do last for six weeks in May and June, with sporadic bloom thereafter. They are, however, small and unprepossessing. The foliage, on the other hand, makes a clump that is somehow both solid and dainty at the same time, providing color and texture contrast with other shade plants.

  Corydalis lutea is a very short-lived perennial, but does freely seed itself, so you need only remove seedlings that spring up where you don't want them. Seedlings reach blooming size rapidly and may even bloom the first fall. Two plants side by side will make an imposing clump that looks like one large plant. I enjoy mine in singles, scattered haphazardly through the border to give an overall lacy appearance to the whole bed.

  These plants prefer rich, moist soil and a half-shaded position. Mine thrive in morning sun and afternoon shade. They are said to be very adaptable, so may fare well for you in shadier spots. They do require good drainage, however, and do not perform well in clay soil when summers are wet.

Phlox divaricata (woodland phlox or wild sweet William), perennial, height eight inches, spread eighteen inches, shade: Low-growing *Phlox divaricata* makes a dandy perennial for the front of a shady border. It does equally well in dry or moist shade, and its pastel lavender-blue flowers really stand out in the dim light of shade, making the plant unusually showy. This slow creeper has lightly fragrant blooms that last a long time—from early May through mid-June. The foliage may develop powdery mildew after the bloom is over, but the plant seems unharmed by simply cutting it back severely and letting surrounding plants take center stage. It doesn't make a very satisfactory cut flower, as it drops its petals almost at once, so leave it in the garden, where it will last and last.

Veronica 'Waterperry' (speedwell), perennial, height four inches, spreading habit, sun: I've grown several highly touted cultivars of *Veronica,* notably *V. spicata* 'Icicle' and *V.* 'Sunny Border Blue,' without success. These perennials do well at first—blooming beautifully and showing great promise. By midsummer of the first or second season the plants begin to show signs of stress from the heat. The leaves brown and curl. With each season they dwindle, looking scrappier and blooming less. By the third year, they are so disreputable that I dig them up and discard them. I have finally concluded that they are just not reliable plants for a hot climate and I no longer waste time, cash, and gardener's guilt on them.

The creeping forms of *Veronica* seem to be the exception, and I particularly like 'Waterperry.' This very low-growing, slowly creeping plant bears tiny, glossy leaves that look as fresh as springtime throughout the growing season, absolutely regardless of the weather. In the summer of 1995, when my garden was sodden with weeks of almost daily rain and then fried in two heat waves of temperatures above 100 degrees, this plant never faltered. The flowers, which appear from early May through early June, are a profuse and pretty light blue with just a hint of lavender. This nice creeping ground cover spreads at a reasonably fast rate without being invasive.

Lamium maculatum (spotted deadnettle), perennial, height four–six inches, spreading habit, shade: You sometimes see *Aegopodium* (bishop's weed, goutweed) recommended as a ground cover for shade or sun, but this is little more than a noxious weed masquerading as a garden perennial. It is very pretty and also relentlessly invasive. Unless you plant it where it is rigidly controlled by such surroundings as buildings, concrete, and mown lawn, bishop's weed will creep into everything and you will rue the day you made its acquaintance. For a perennial ground cover with the same look of shimmering green and white in shade, plant *Lamium maculatum* instead. This polite plant spreads fairly rapidly, but is easily uprooted when it goes where you don't want it. *L. maculatum* 'Beacon Silver,' with mauve-pink flowers, is commonly available, but I prefer white-blooming 'White Nancy,' which seems to fill in better and has a frostier look. On both of these the bloom is insignificant and not particularly noticeable. 'Pink Pewter,' on the other hand, has slightly larger, far showier blooms in a very appealing clear pink. It flowers from mid-May right on through to frost, making it a charming addition to a shade garden. Also worth trying is *L. maculatum* 'Aureum,' syn. 'Gold Leaf' with acid yellow foliage that makes gorgeous pools of light in shade. It is not as vigorous or as quick to spread as other spotted deadnettles and prefers a shadier location. All of these are good weavers, working their way around nearby plants without threatening their existence. 'White Nancy' is beautiful at the feet of *Pulmonaria* 'Roy Davidson' in one part of my garden. In another, it forms a puddle of light beneath a shaded bench. Spotted deadnettle is well suited to moderate to heavy shade. In light shade or part shade, it will suffer during heat waves.

Dicentra spectabilis (bleeding heart), perennial, height twenty-four to thirty-six inches, spread twenty-four to forty-eight inches, shade to part sun: I confess to harboring tender feelings toward bleeding heart, which I consider one of the loveliest plants available. The pink and white flowers are like a row of ballerinas dangling by their toes from gracefully arched stalks. The leaves are deeply cut and a soft blue-green color. This perennial dies to the ground in fall, but grows rapidly in spring to form a shrublike presence in the garden by early May, when it begins to bloom. *Dicentra spectabilis* can be grown in a variety of shade to part sun conditions. In sunnier spots it often goes dormant with the arrival of hot weather. When the leaves begin to yellow, just cut the plant to the ground and let other plants fill in around it. In shade it shows its lovely foliage at least into August, and in cooler summers until frost. Bleeding heart blooms throughout May into June.

In addition to *D. spectabilis* with its pink flowers, I also grow *D. spectabilis* f. *alba,* a striking plant that never fails to elicit comment from garden visitors. The white blooms have a special elegance and purity that looks somehow classic. The foliage is paler and less blue and the plant has a much longer bloom season if spent blossoms are cut promptly. It begins flowering the first of May and may continue into September. If you leave the blooms on and let the plant go to seed you can easily increase your stock (I have never had the pink form of bleeding heart self-seed in my garden, however).

I've also grown *D. eximia* 'Alba,' which I found very disappointing. Its diminutive size (about eight inches high and eight inches wide) makes it easy to overlook. The blossoms, too, are shaped more like a kernel of corn than a ballerina and their small size and number make them insignificant. There is quite a lot of noise made in the nursery trade about long-blooming cultivars of *D. eximia* like 'Luxuriant.' Their color and bloom form is so inferior to the original that I see nothing to recommend them. Length of bloom isn't everything.

Aquilegia (columbine), perennial, size varies, shade to part sun: It's difficult to think of a group of shade garden plants more enticing than the columbines. These refined perennial beauties have many charms. The foliage is very good-looking—rounded and bluish with scalloped edges. The unique two-part flowers show a face formed of five cups. Graceful spurs shoot backward. The flower may be nodding or face outward. Columbines have a long season of bloom, too, each kind flowering for about six weeks in spring and early summer.

The plant has a very free seeding habit, though it is a matter of opinion whether this is a positive or a negative. On the one hand, it is useful since columbines tend to be short-lived and the on-coming seedlings are ready to fill vacancies as older plants die off. On the other hand, columbines are promiscuous and cultivars and species cross with abandon. If you have a particular color you love and wish to keep true, do not plant any other sort nearby. The two will cross and recross until you have every possible variation on the two parents. Each plant forms a large amount of seed, so your shade garden in spring is likely to be carpeted with seedlings. It's wise to weed these down to just a few, because columbines do not appreciate crowding.

Columbine seed, by the way, must go through a winter before it will germinate. Purchased seed will be ready to plant, but if you are given seed from a friend's garden, either plant it in the fall or store it in the freezer until spring.

Unfortunately, along with their charms, columbines have a pair of serious weak points. They are quite likely to be attacked by fungus and leaf miner. In the maggot form, leaf miner eats its way through leaf surfaces, leaving a clearly identifiable winding white trail. You will never see the insect itself, but the white trail is a dead giveaway. You can remove affected leaves as soon as you see them, and it's a good idea to clear away all foliage in the autumn—this should be destroyed, not added to the compost pile. You can treat leaf miner with a spray, but it is also deadly to bees and other useful insects. The truth is that even if you are so reckless of your garden ecology as to use this insecticide, you will probably not get rid of the leaf miner.

Fungus is likely to attack columbines in mid- to late summer, disfiguring the leaves with gray spots. You can treat the plants with fungicide, but it will not be fully effective. In my opinion, your best bet is to remove and destroy all foliage when it begins to look unsightly. The plant will soon create new leaves. Columbines prefer a rich, moist soil with good drainage. They will be less subject to fungus attack if they are kept adequately moist, but they don't want to sit in water. This means providing them with light to moderate shade and soil rich in organic matter and then watering on a regular basis. They are often recommended for full sun, but will not fare well in such siting in our region. Give them light shade for best results.

The more columbines you plant in close proximity, the more trouble you will have with both fungus and leaf miner, so it's a good idea to limit their number. One type that seems less likely to be attacked by these two problems is *A. canadensis,* the wild columbine seen in the Midwest that is also known as Canada columbine. At about three feet, this is a tall plant, but the loose arrangement of stems and blossoms in its narrow eighteen-inch width gives it an overall airy appearance. The forward, cup-shaped part of the flower is pink to coral pink, the spur portion pale yellow. The nodding blooms last from about the first week in May through mid-June, with slight bloom well into July. A favorite cultivar is *A. canadensis* 'Corbett,' a solid little clump that covers itself in small, pendulous, pale yellow flowers for a long period. Plants stand about twenty to twenty-four inches high and eighteen inches across. 'Corbett' blooms from mid-May until mid-June. In my garden it has not yet fallen victim to either leaf miner or fungus.

If you've admired *A. caerulea,* the Rocky Mountain columbine, on mountain vacations, you can plant it in your own garden. It has white, upward facing cups with sky blue spurs. It is very lovely, though not as heavenly in the hot Midwest as it looks in rarefied mountain air.

Geranium (cranesbill), perennial, size varies, sun to light shade:
Those pungently scented plants with large, richly red blooms,
commonly grown in containers, treated as annuals, and known
as "geraniums," are actually members of the *Pelargonium* genus.
The plants in the genus *Geranium* I'm recommending here are
perennials—far more subtle plants with smaller leaves and blossoms. Though often suggested for full sun, they fare better in light
shade in our climate. They are more interesting than showy, with
flowers that are pleasant but not striking or profuse, and a cut
leaf shape and rough texture that provide good contrast.

There are lots of species and cultivars to choose from, so if geraniums appeal to you, just start trying them. I like *Geranium*
'Johnson's Blue' for its purple-blue flowers that seem to shimmer
with a slight underlying pink. The plants spread at a moderate rate
and are a bit loose and gangly, so they look best weaving in among
plants with more solidity of form. When in bloom, from mid-May
through the end of June, they form sprawling clumps eight to
fourteen inches high. *G.* x *magnificum,* with a purple flower, is a
suitable substitute for a more solid, upright form.

G. sanguineum var. *striatum,* syn. *G. sanguineum* var. *lancastriense* is low growing with small leaves. Plants are six or eight
inches tall and slowly spreading. Pale pink flowers appear sporadically throughout summer and fall, but make their best show
in spring. The flowering season is from the end of May until a
week or so before frost.

I enjoy *G. phaeum* (mourning widow) as an oddity. Its small,
dark purple flowers are held high above loose and casual foliage.
When in flower it stands twenty to twenty-four inches high and
twenty inches across. When the blooms fade and stalks are cut
back, the basal foliage is eight inches tall. It requires a reasonably
moist location and does well in my garden in the shade of a pine
tree. Flowering is from mid-May through mid-July.

Convallaria (lily-of-the-valley), perennial, height eight inches, spread five–six inches, shade: Who can resist the blandishments of lily-of-the-valley? This perennial's name alone recommends it. The lavishly fragrant blossoms are perfectly described in that old round song: "White coral bells upon a slender stalk." The broad, basal, ovate leaves look attractive all summer in a shady location, their smooth quality contrasting handsomely with a more textured foliage like *Astilbe chinensis* var. *pumila* (false spirea), *Geranium,* or *Athyrium niponicum* (Japanese painted fern). In autumn the leaves turn a nice gold. Sometimes categorized as a bulb, *Convallaria* actually grows from thick rhizomes.

Once planted in a moist spot, in moderate to heavy shade, lily-of-the-valley requires no further care and nurturing. The plants may begin rather slowly, but in two or three years, they will fill in and start to spread. Eventually you will need to exercise control as they begin to creep beyond their allotted space, sometimes into unlikely spots like the scant quarter inch between a brick patio and a house. This spreading habit gives them a nice, snug, tucked-in look among other plants. A light mulch of compost or manure will increase bloom size.

Though the bloom, which begins in the middle of May, is brief, a handful of the flowers bunched into a small vase on the kitchen windowsill for a few days each spring is reason enough to include them in your shady garden.

Galium odoratum, syn. *Asperula odorata* (sweet woodruff), perennial, height six–eight inches, spreading habit, shade: Sweet woodruff is a delicately pretty ground cover with whorls of dark green leaves. Its spring bloom is lovely but brief, lasting only about three weeks at the end of May. The flowers are tiny and white. Although the whole plant is said to be fragrant, don't count on its scent to be a feature of your garden unless you're willing to crawl on your hands and knees, stick your nose to the ground, and crush the plant to enjoy it. Sweet woodruff's strong point is its foliage. This perennial spreads at a moderate rate, but may take two or three years to take hold. Avoid planting it around low perennials, as they may be swamped by the sweet woodruff. Once established, it weaves cozily in among its neighbors, creating the sort of no-dirt-showing garden that is so particularly appealing. Plant sweet woodruff in moderate to heavy shade. Shear it back after it flowers for a fresh regrowth of foliage.

Tiarella wherryi, syn. *T. cordifolia* var. *collina* (Wherry's foamflower), perennial, shade, height eight–ten inches, spread eight inches: *Tiarella cordifolia* (foamflower) is a pretty little perennial wildflower that rapidly spreads by stolons (horizontal branches from the plant base that spread underground, taking root) to become a pretty little pest. Choose instead *T. wherryi*, which may go to seed on a modest scale—handy for increasing your stock—but is not stoloniferous. It thrives in shade.

    This small perennial's bloom is not especially eye-catching or imposing. The little inverted cone of several tiny flowers is creamy white dusted with soft rose. Avoid placing it near a plant of pure white in leaf or flower, where it will look dull and dirty. To create a show, plant *T. wherryi* in groups of at least a half dozen as a companion to hostas or other smooth-leafed plants. The heart-shaped light green leaves with darker serrated edges will contrast beautifully with their neighbors throughout the season. The flowers occur from mid-May until late June.

Baptisia australis (blue wild indigo, false indigo, or plains false indigo), perennial, height forty-eight inches, spread forty-eight inches, sun or light shade: What first attracted me to *Baptisia australis* was the lovely blue of its unusual pea-like flowers. I saw it in bloom in a friend's yard and fell in love. My friend gave me some seeds, and three years later I had a sizable blooming perennial plant. Garden visitors always love it and comment on its pretty flowers, but blue wild indigo has a short bloom season—only about two weeks at the end of May and the beginning of June. What you need to admire if you are going to put this one in your garden are the foliage and form. The oval leaves are a bluish shade that makes for nice contrast with everyday green, and the plant form is quite shrublike.

Blue wild indigo gets larger with each year, so once it reaches and then exceeds the size you want, you need to divide it. The tough mass of roots make this a challenge, and success with transplanted pieces may be mixed. A plant about five years old will be four feet high with an arching vase shape that is roughly four feet across. You can tame the beast by pruning it back hard after bloom, cutting back about half of the growth. The plant will take up less space in the garden when not in bloom and will increase in size more slowly. There is a dwarf variety available for smaller gardens. Blue wild indigo grows very well in full sun, never showing any stress from hot, dry conditions. It is also adaptable for partial shade.

If you are given seeds, be sure to scarify them before planting. I poured boiling water on mine and soaked them overnight. Then with the outer shell of the seed softened, I used a paring knife to carefully nick the coating, making it easier for the seed to sprout.

Heuchera (coral flower or coral bells), perennial, height six–eight inches, spread eight inches, sun or part shade: With a low cluster of scalloped leaves and a myriad of long wiry bloom stalks topped by clusters of tiny bell-shaped pink flowers, coral bells do much to give the early summer garden a look of airy bounty. I planted them in pairs at intervals along the front of a sunny border. When they flower from the last week in May through the middle of July, they tie the whole bed together.

Coral bells are perennial and seem to be unaffected by pests or diseases, but siting is critical. They do not generally fare well in the direct rays of a Midwestern sun. They prefer rich, moist soil in light shade, where they will live longer, bloom better, and have healthier foliage than they will in full sun. Even in the shade, some of them will not last long or look good in our climate. There are exceptions, though. In my sunny border I grow *Heuchera* x *brizoides* 'Chatterbox,' which seems to positively glory in its hot and glaring location. In "Coralbells Get a New Look" published in *Fine Gardening* magazine (November–December 1995, 48–53), Dan Heims recommends three others for sun: *H. americana* 'Garnet,' *H.* 'Strawberry Swirl,' and *H.* 'Winter Red.' Unless a cultivar is specifically suggested for full sun, you'd better stick with light shade.

The pink flowers vary from a muted dusty rose to fiery hot pink. Of those cultivars I have tried, the more muted flowers seemed to grow on the stronger, longer-lived plants. Perhaps this is a coincidence, but much as I love the brilliant pinks, none of these plants has done really well for me. Although the softer pinks may be somewhat less appealing, the mass of bloom created by a couple of plants side by side is most impressive. Even at second best, they are too wonderful to be spared from your garden.

Breeders are now creating cultivars of *Heuchera* with pale green or green-and-white-streaked leaves. These are ideal for lighting up a shady spot and seem well worth investigating. I grow one of the variegated plants called 'Snow Angel,' which seems oblivious to heat. *Heuchera micrantha* var. *diversifolia* 'Palace Purple' has pointed leaves of a dark purplish brown. This leaf color recedes in the shade, so careful placement is important. They are gorgeous combined with chartreuse hostas.

Nepeta (catmint), perennial, size varies, sun: A favorite plant in my garden is *Nepeta* x *faassenii,* syn. *N. mussinii* of gardens. I started it from seeds purchased almost twenty years ago and have divided this perennial and spread it around my garden until its presence scattered along the front edge has become a unifying feature. Garden literature suggests that this plant seeds itself freely, but I haven't found this to be true.

N. x *faassenii* forms a low-growing, soft clump. Its leaves are small, nicely textured, and gray green. The blooms are a hazy lavender blue, not individually showy, but the whole plant has an air of misty delicacy that softens the edges of a garden quite beautifully. It is especially nice grown around the base of roses or clematis or up against any plant that seems too bare at its feet. If you love the way lavender looks in books but have been disappointed in its lack of vigor in our climate, try catmint instead for its similar leaf color, bloom color, romantic look, and general shape and size. Catmint is of the weaver persuasion, making its way in among its neighbors and nicely covering naked earth. The best gardens are those where plants run all together, leaving no visible bare earth around them, and this plant is a good sort for helping to accomplish that look.

Catmint forms a dome-shaped clump that will collapse outward in the first heavy rain or sudden heat. The plant will then grow new foliage at the center to fill in neatly. *N.* x *faassenii* grows about one foot high and two feet across, making it a good choice to spill over the front edge of a border. If you like the look of catmint but want something a bit more stately and substantial, try *N.* 'Six Hills Giant.' Described in most garden books as a three-foot-tall erect plant, this catmint in my garden is more like two feet tall and flopping. This may be due to Farm Belt heat, but a friend who grows her 'Six Hills Giant' in poorer soil has somewhat better results. I have had improved luck getting it to grow upright with thorough and early pea staking.

I'm talking here, by the way, about catmint and not catnip (*N. cataria*). Cats, of course, are known to roll around in catnip until they are positively looped. This destructive behavior does not seem to extend to the ornamental catmints that I have grown. Although my neighborhood rejoices in an extensive population of cats, I have never seen any besotted tomfoolery directed at my catmint.

Cut catmint back in early spring, about six weeks before the frost-free date, to three or four inches from the ground. The plants will come up nicely and bloom from late May into mid-July. Then shear the plant back by about half. It looks a bit hacked for a couple of weeks, but new growth quickly begins to fill in and give it a nice bushy look again. The plant will then bloom sporadically for the rest of the growing season.

Early Summer

Iris, perennial, height varies, spreading, sun: The genus *Iris* has about three hundred species and many, many cultivars divided into a few groupings. When people speak of irises, they're usually talking about tall bearded irises, perennials of great beauty. A healthy and vigorous tall bearded iris at the peak of its bloom is a glorious sight. The blooms are as thrillingly exotic as orchids. The light coming through them in the late afternoon turns the flowers to jewels. With three or five or even more big beautiful blooms on each stalk, they can take your breath away. People who love irises become obsessed, possessed by their rich beauty. My mother is in this category. At the height of her garden life, she had 350 different kinds and was still hungry for more. Her garden at the peak of the iris bloom was a wonderland.

On the flip side, though, many gardeners detest tall bearded irises, and with good reason. First, the flowering period is short. Each plant blooms for about ten days to two weeks, with the entire season spanning only about three weeks from mid-May until the end of the first week in June. While they bloom they are gorgeous, but let's talk about the other thirty-two weeks of the growing season. Their foliage is a light, silvery green that is attractive when healthy, especially when rain makes quicksilver droplets along the leaves. Unfortunately, healthy iris foliage is rarely around for long. The plants require excellent drainage. Without it they are subject to rot, which turns their underpinnings to mush. Even in thoroughly prepared, loose soil, many of mine rotted in the rainy spring of 1995. The foliage is also prey to various leaf spots that disfigure it and can kill the plants. If that isn't discouraging enough, consider the larva of the iris borer, which will enter rhizomes and eat them relentlessly down to a hollow shell.

If you love the tall beardeds, you must deal with these problems. This requires an organized preventive spraying program that would make an organic gardener flinch. When the tulips bloom you will need to start spraying your irises with a fungicide. Spraying should continue (except during bloom time) throughout the growing season. I cannot bring myself to introduce this much spraying into my garden, so I take more natural, less effective measures. As the leaves die or become seriously diseased, I remove and destroy them. I never put any part of the plant into my compost heap. One year when my iris foliage was a mess from leaf spot, I got radical, cutting it all back to the ground and destroying it. The plants put up new leaves and looked better for the rest of the season than they ever had before.

If a plant falls victim to iris borer, dig it up. Break the rhizome apart but leave a fan of leaves attached to each piece. Choose the strongest-looking rhizome and cut off any flower stalk. Cut the foliage back to about five or six inches long. You will wind up with a small fan of trimmed leaves attached to a large rhizome with perhaps a few smaller rhizomes branching off it and a few roots. Discard the remainder of the plant. Wearing rubber gloves, submerge the fan in a bucket of nine parts water and one part bleach plus a fungicide mixed according to package directions. Soak the fan for thirty minutes. Then rinse the plant with a hose and leave it to dry fully in a shady spot before replanting it.

Irises must be planted high. Dig a shallow hole and enrich the soil with superphosphate and bonemeal. Add a small amount of lime, too, since irises do not like an acidic soil. Now mound some of the loose dirt in the center of the hole. Put the iris fan on the mound and fill in with dirt so that the roots are well covered, but the thick rhizome is only barely covered. Some books advise you to leave the top of the rhizome exposed, but I find that this usually results in the plant being pulled out by the first curious squirrel. The base of the leaves must definitely not be covered with dirt.

The iris will gradually grow around, forming a ring of rhizomes and their leaf fans. Once the ring is solid, the rhizomes will begin to be overcrowded and bloom will diminish. At this point, probably after three to five years, you need to dig and divide the plant as described above. It's a good idea to treat it with the bleach and fungicide soak, too.

In spite of all their problems, I do grow several irises because I love their sweet scent. In a good year I enjoy their glories. In a bad year I live with the mess. My favorite is a pastel pink called *I.* 'Vanity' that has an orange beard, large blossoms, and a long bloom period. It is always the first to bloom in my garden and outlasts several that start later. Another good one is *I.* 'Gold Galore,' which is simply the richest, most luscious gold color I've ever seen in a flower.

I once asked my mother which tall bearded iris cultivars she would choose if she could grow only five. She listed 'Vanity,' 'Victoria Falls,' 'Pink Swan,' 'Bubbling Over,' and 'Stepping Out.' After producing this list fairly quickly, she went on to say that she would hate to give up 'Smoke Rings,' 'Sapphire Hills,' 'Persian Berry,' 'Margarita,' 'Gigolo,' 'Mystique,' 'Gay Parasol,' 'Going My Way,' 'Gold Galore,' 'Fort Apache,' 'Conch Call,' 'Copper Classic,' 'Color Splash,' 'Cherry Smoke,' 'Camelot Rose,' and 'Snow Mound.' She went on adding to the list over the next few days until the recitation of her favorites began to sound like a complete iris catalog. Did I mention that some gardeners become obsessed with the tall bearded iris?

For my money the Siberian iris is a better choice for the heat and humidity of the Midwest. This delightful perennial's blooms resemble a flight of butterflies. In fact, one Siberian cultivar bears that name. Though Siberians flower for a relatively short period of time, perhaps only two weeks in late May or early June, their foliage and strong vertical line make them a handsome addition to the perennial garden. The clump of long silvery leaves remains tall, elegant, cool, and attractive throughout the summer and seems impervious to heat, drought, excessive rain, wind, and fungus. In fall the leaves turn a tawny gold, beautiful in sunlight.

Siberians have been so widely hybridized that a seemingly endless selection is available to choose from. You may find a limited choice (or none at all) at local nurseries, but catalogs offer an enormous and bewildering range.

One you may be able to find locally is *Iris* 'Caesar's Brother.' This majestic plant forms a large, vigorous clump, stiffly upright and exceptionally tall. The plant is about three feet high with the profuse, deep blue-violet blooms held another six inches above the foliage. The vivid color adds a piquant note among the more common pastels of this early season. Following bloom the leaves are less strongly vertical, arching gracefully.

I. 'White Swirl' is somewhat smaller with an exquisite flower—delicate and pure white. The lower petals stand out horizontally. The bloom stalks and leaves have a slight tendency to fall over, but the overall effect of the plant is still very pleasing. Use pea staking to prop the plant or position it between sturdy neighbors. Or you can just cut the blooms that flop over for indoor bouquets. Flowering is so profuse that they won't be missed.

Another Siberian that I particularly love is *I.* 'Ego.' The plant is relatively small and its blooms are less profuse than those of either 'Caesar's Brother' or 'White Swirl,' but the color is a thrilling sapphire blue that will stop you in your tracks. I give starts of this one to only my very best friends.

Siberians are generally easy to divide and transplant, though the older, more established clumps are not easy to dig and lift because they are large and heavy. This is a plant you can buy just one of and then divide repeatedly every other year or so to build your stock.

Athyrium niponicum, syn. *A. goeringianum* (Japanese painted fern), perennial, height eighteen inches, spread eighteen inches, shade: Japanese painted fern doesn't flower, so it's difficult to know where to include it in a list of plants arranged chronologically by bloom, but I'll throw it in here, because by early summer the leaves are fully developed and showy. This is quite simply one of the most beautiful plants in my garden. It thrives in the shade of pines or deciduous trees, and is lovely planted with columbines, hostas, lily-of-the-valley, or lungwort. It is especially nice combined with the markedly bluish *Hosta* 'Krossa Regal.' It is relatively low growing and its leaf color is a shimmering mix of green, frosty blue, white, and a suggestion of pink. It has the opalescence of abalone shell and really must be seen to be believed. Grown in the rich, deep soil you can make by mixing plenty of compost into your dirt, it gets about eighteen inches tall. In poorer rocky or sandy soil, it is more of a ground hugger. By late summer heat will take its toll, making the fronds collapse.

Stachys byzantina, syn. *S. lanata* (lamb's-ears), perennial, height twelve inches, spreading habit, sun: This beautiful foliage plant has thick, soft, downy gray leaves that are very attractive placed along the front of a border. They appear fresh and firm in spring, but on the arrival of summer heat and humidity, they droop, rot, and become unsightly. Their unusual bloom spikes of mauve-lavender tubular flowers almost submerged in gray foliage are more interesting than lovely. Heavy or continued rains will knock flower stalks down and plaster the leaves into the mud. The plant is quite nice seen at its best, but in the Midwest where heat, humidity, and summer thunderstorms will take their toll, it is a less than desirable addition to the perennial border. Fortunately, there is a sturdy cultivar called 'Wave Hill' that does not bloom and whose foliage stands up to our weather very well. Give it a try for a nice splash of silver. It spreads moderately rapidly to form a nice ground cover, and it's easy to increase for edging a garden. Tidy it up in spring by removing the dead foliage of the previous season.

Alchemilla mollis (lady's mantle), perennial, height eight inches, spread fifteen inches, light to moderate shade: If you have a shady area in your garden, run (do not walk) to your nearest garden shop to buy *Alchemilla mollis.* Or, better yet, beg the seeds from a gardening friend, as it starts easily from seed, making a full-size blooming perennial plant in the second season. You have no doubt admired it in gardening books for its profuse sprays of tiny, sulfur yellow flowers and its crimped leaves with their pinked edges. The foliage is uniquely formed to catch rain or heavy dew, which rings each leaf with beads of moisture. The stylish leaves, delicate bloom, fresh color, and billowy form make it a must for the romantic look. It is one of those wonderfully touching plants that you find yourself adoring as if it were a kitten or a baby.

Lady's mantle definitely requires a shady spot in our climate. I foolishly planted several in an enclosed garden where they received sun for only about six hours a day, but they soon made it clear that this was too much. Though the plants continued to thrive, the leaves took on a dry and scorched look in summer. They fared better when moved to a shadier site.

The buds appear in late May, giving lady's mantle an illusion of bloom even before the flowering starts about a week later. Bloom continues through mid-July. After bloom, you can cut back the foliage to allow fresh new leaves to take over.

Allium schoenoprasum (chives), perennial, height eighteen inches, spread twelve inches, sun: You know what chives are: you chop them up in salads or stir them into hash-brown potatoes. Relatives of the culinary onion, they are commonly recommended for herb gardens. I think they have a place in the perennial border as well.

Chives are bulbous, each bulb with several leaves, and the bulbs growing together in tight little packs. The leaves are tubular and tapered, like long thick blades of grass. These well-behaved plants spread only very slowly. When you want to reduce or increase your supply, just dig up the clump, divide it with a shovel, and plant or discard the pieces.

The flowers are globe shaped and a soft lavender, lasting a full six weeks from the end of June until the middle of July. They are as ornamental as anything else in flower in the garden at this point, so why not plant them among your late tulips, catmint, irises, coral bells, and roses? After they bloom, the leaves will collapse and become unsightly. When the bloom starts to fade, just shear back the entire plant to near the ground and let new growth shoot up. They soon fill in beautifully. Once the fresh growth comes on, you'll be able to harvest chives for the kitchen—a nice little bonus. Don't disfigure the plant by chopping a small amount off across the whole top. Instead, select just a few leaves and cut off whatever you need near ground level.

Rosa (rose), perennial, size varies, sun: Let me first admit that I know relatively little about roses. Whole books have been written on the hundreds and hundreds of cultivars. Read one or two if you plan to add roses to your garden. Roses are well known for their propensity to become diseased and look dreadful. I didn't even attempt a rose until I had been gardening for a dozen years. Now, after more than twenty, I am just beginning to have the nerve to try several. I regret the wasted years of timidity, too, because nothing adds to the romantic look of a garden like roses. Roses are also fabulous cut flowers and nothing matches their scent.

The kind you most often see are hybrid tea roses. The blooms, which appear repeatedly all summer, are elegantly beautiful. The bushes, however, are not particularly attractive, and they are subject to black spot, powdery mildew, and other diseases. On many, the scent is modest to insignificant. These are the roses with which I was chiefly familiar in my youth and early gardening years. I enjoyed them in other people's gardens, but saw that they required a time-consuming amount of spraying and babying along, and I simply devoted my garden space to less demanding flowers.

On a garden tour of England several years ago, I happened to see Sissinghurst, Hidcote, and other famous gardens at the absolute peak of their late spring bloom when the old roses were in full flower. I was almost literally swept away by the heady fragrance of several of these roses planted in an enclosed garden. It was a powerful lesson in the importance of scent in creating an atmosphere of magical sanctuary. On top of their fragrance, these roses had substantial size in both shrub and flower. They were simply the most billowing, romantic, powerful flowers I had ever encountered. Their only apparent drawback was that they bloomed just once a year.

I returned home yearning to grow them in my own garden, but unable to see where I had space for them. Meanwhile, I began to read about David Austin's English roses. Austin is an English rose breeder who has been crossing old garden roses with hybrid teas and floribundas. By doing so, he has been able to introduce over eighty cultivars that offer the best traits of each. From the old roses they take their large full flowers, heavy fragrance, handsome shrubby form, vigor, and disease resistance. From the moderns, they take their color range and repeat bloom. This seemed like the best of both worlds to me, so when I created an enclosed garden at one side of my house, I framed the gate with a pair of David Austin rose bushes—*Rosa* 'Mary Rose.'

'Mary Rose' is generally described as growing to about four feet tall and four feet across. A friend who owns a local nursery raises this rose at her acreage outside of town, where weather conditions are severe. For her, it reaches only about two and a half to three feet in height. In my enclosed garden in town, planted against a fence with a southern exposure, this rose is a behemoth. Even with drastic pruning throughout the season, it still tops out well over six feet by late autumn. It blooms heavily in spring, beginning about the end of May and continuing until late June. It then takes a brief vacation—three or four weeks—before beginning a period of lighter bloom that lasts from mid-July through late October. This adds up to an impressive sixteen weeks of bloom. The fragrance, which its breeder assesses at only one star (of a possible three), is strong, peppery, and sweet. Though the evident variability in the size of this particular rose gave me pause, I decided to try another David Austin rose.

R. 'Sharifa Asma' is a small rose, just two and a half or three feet tall. The scent is delicious and the shell pink flowers are very beautiful. With lesser calamint and *Geranium sanguineum* var. *striatum* planted at its feet it is truly lovely. In its first year, planted as a mere stick, it bloomed from mid-July until frost.

Much as I love my David Austins, I can't say that I've found them to be completely disease free. When heat and humidity strike they may require spraying for powdery mildew and black spot.

I can also recommend a shrub rose called *R.* 'Bonica.' Though described in books as reaching three feet high and three feet across, after several years in my garden, it grew to about four and a half feet high. 'Bonica' has glossy leaves relatively untroubled by disease. The small, shell-pink flowers appear in sprays so that you can cut one stem and have a miniature bouquet. They are especially lovely in bud. Although this rose blooms continually from mid-June until frost, the heaviest bloom occurs in the first three weeks.

For beautiful foliage you can't beat *Rosa glauca,* syn. *R. rubrifolia* with its bluish leaves, reddish stems, and graceful fountain shape. It grows tall, about six feet, with a spread of four feet or more. Bright pink single flowers appear for just a week in early to mid-June, but the foliage is beautiful all summer and yellow hips gradually turn orange in fall.

Roses like a rich, well-drained soil and plenty of water. Water them gently at the base and avoid wetting the leaves. To promote vigor and bloom, use a liquid rose fertilizer according to package instructions. When the plants become diseased you will have to spray because they don't heal themselves. Seek advice at a good nursery.

Lychnis coronaria (rose campion), biennial or short-lived perennial, height twenty-four inches, spread eighteen inches, sun: The velvety silver foliage of *Lychnis coronaria* contrasts beautifully with darker greens and is reason enough to grow it. This is one plant that can stand up to full sun in our region, but it also manages well in very light shade or in full sun with some afternoon shade. The branching stems bear flowers in snowy white or very dark rose (magenta). The plant blooms from the second week in June through August at least.

Deadheading encourages continued bloom, but be warned: it is a big job because this plant is a profuse bloomer. Rose campion goes to seed with enthusiasm, so if you don't want it to take over, you must remove seed heads or hoe out the small plants as the seeds germinate. This propensity for self-sowing is useful since the plants are short-lived, often lasting just two years. If the plant stops blooming and the foliage begins to look ratty, just pull it up and discard it. Let the seed it has scattered germinate for next year's bloom. Rose campion does not take especially well to transplanting, so plant seed directly in the garden and move any seedlings that require relocation while they are quite small.

Achillea 'Moonshine' (yarrow), perennial, height twelve–eighteen inches, spreading habit, sun: Trying to get a gardener to name a favorite flower is like trying to get a mother to choose her favorite child. Still, if pressed, I might name this standout perennial. Its leaves, like fern fronds painted a silvery sage green, are enough alone to put it on a list of beloved perennials. The bloom heads—flat clusters of tiny flowers—are a shade of yellow so pure and lemony that even the glare of the Midwestern sun can't steal its freshness. In early spring the leaves of *Achillea* 'Moonshine' sparkle with dew or raindrops. In late spring they send up numerous bloom stalks that continue to flower through August.

When the color fades from the flowers, cut them back to encourage a second, less showy and less prolific bloom. After the second bloom fades, cut that back, too, and you still have gorgeous foliage. This remains a pleasurable sight even in winter when frost limns its lacy edges. I can't think of another perennial that is beautiful over so long a stretch.

The only drawback of *Achillea* 'Moonshine' is minor: It weakens as it rapidly increases, making division desirable at least every other year. Frequent division will keep its clump form neater and encourage bloom. Left alone, the plant will grow side clumps and become twiggy and less attractive. On the upside, the roots are not deep and the plant parts are easily distinguished and separated. This perennial is drought tolerant, but will wilt badly if divided in hot weather. Divide in fall when weather cools (late

August or later), or early in spring, four to six weeks ahead of the frost-free date. Water the divisions carefully until they take hold.

Clematis, perennial vine, size varies, sun: The large genus *Clematis* is made up of climbers that dress up walls and fences and drape themselves across gateways, doing much to create a lush ambiance. Some are very vigorous and reliable, while others—at least in our area—are disappointingly spindly and anemic year after year. When planting them, remember the old saw that clematis vines like their feet in the shade and their heads in the sun. Give them a sunny location, but shade their root runs with something low and bushy growing at the base, such as catmint. This foundation plant needs to be up and providing cooling shade before hot weather strikes. Plant clematis in rich, deep soil with plenty of organic matter and a half cup of lime. All these vines will need a trellis to ascend, because they climb by winding leaf stems around something. If it's a bit of a stretch from the ground to the bottom of the trellis, jam a few twigs into the earth to give the vine a boost.

Widely in use in the Midwest and very reliable is *C.* x *jackmanii,* which has a strong climbing habit and showers of big purple blossoms in early to midsummer. If you think this is an overused clematis, remember that it is so common because it is so reliable. As often as I see it, I still think that a simple mailbox on a post smothered in this vine is a thoroughly charming sight.

If you want to go for something less widely used, try *C. lanuginosa* 'Candida.' The blooms are very large and flat, about six or seven inches across, and pure, gleaming white. Flowering lasts a full month from the second week in June until mid-July. I also like *C. viticella* (not hardy in zone 4), with its small reddish-purple blooms, each petal twisted slightly. Prune it close to ground level in April. The flowering is profuse and lasting and the vine is vigorous. Let it grow over an arbor so you can look up into its dangling flowers. This one will be in full bloom from mid-June through the end of the first week in July, with some continuation of minor flowering.

A favorite is the fall bloomer called sweet autumn clematis and confusingly named *C. terniflora* or *C. maximowicziana* or *C. paniculata* depending on whose catalog you're perusing. Whatever you call it, it covers itself in small starry white flowers whose fragrance can knock you down from several feet away. The yellow stamens give the flowers a slightly off-white look. Unfortunately, the bloom is brief—only about two weeks in the early half of September. Prune it to one to three feet from the ground four to six weeks before the frost-free date in spring.

The variety of clematis out there waiting to be tried is truly staggering. I suggest watching out for sales late in the spring and then trying several to see what happens. If you get serious about clematis, it's worth buying a book on them, because correct pruning requirements vary.

Digitalis (foxglove), size varies, shade: Foxgloves are those graceful towers of large bells that grow wild in wooded areas of England and always look spectacular pictured in a perennial border. They can't stand winds without staking, will desiccate and topple in heat, and thrive in cool, moist conditions. They do not fare well in our climate. I include the members of this large genus here only because for some gardeners, foxgloves are irresistible. If you are one of the stricken, I offer a few tips for the quixotic task of raising foxgloves in the hot and windy Midwest.

Most foxgloves are biennials—in other words, they live just two years. You grow them from seed one year and they flower, set seed, and die the next year. The plants seldom live beyond the second season. For years I grew foxgloves in my shade border with mixed results. They survived milder winters reasonably well and were statuesque and lovely the following spring. When winters were harsh (i.e., typical), all or nearly all of them would be dead by spring. I grew *D. purpurea* 'Excelsior,' a pretty cultivar of common foxglove that stood four to five feet tall. I also tried a number of others from seed with very little success. As thrillingly beautiful as the foxgloves were when they performed well, their inconsistency was maddeningly disappointing and the gigantic holes left in the garden by the many that died were disastrous.

There is a purportedly annual foxglove, *D. purpurea* 'Foxy,' which is meant to bloom in late summer of its first year from seed. I have grown it twice from seed and bought nursery sets once and never saw any bloom. The foliage did well and by summer's end the plants were large enough to flower, but no bloom appeared. The following spring they were dead.

A relative newcomer in my garden is *D.* x *mertonensis,* a perennial foxglove commonly called strawberry foxglove. Shorter than the sort you see in photos of English country house gardens, it is still pretty and flowers a long time, starting in mid-June. When it finishes, you can cut off the main bloom and side blooms will appear and last into mid-August. The color is a nice mauve pink that looks very soft but is often misleadingly described as crushed strawberry. The leaves are heavily textured, large, and quite beautiful in their own right. *D.* x *mertonensis* lived through one typical Nebraska winter only to die the following winter when temperatures yo-yoed from 50 degrees to -10.

Another modestly successful foxglove for the Midwest is *D. lutea* (straw foxglove). Its pale yellow, tubular flowers are much smaller and stiffer than those of *D.* x *mertonensis* or *D. purpurea* 'Excelsior,' which are soft and dangling. Still, it is a taking little thing that always attracts notice from visitors. The plant is perennial and freely self-sows, so you can expand your colony readily. In my garden, *D. lutea* lived through several winters only to turn up their toes en masse during the aforementioned killer winter. Another perennial foxglove worth trying is *D. grandiflora,* syn. *D. ambigua,* a taller yellow-flowered foxglove.

All foxgloves require rich moist soil. Give them plenty of humus, water them in, and make sure the soil stays moist. If they are inadequately moist, the taller stalks will weaken until the weight of the flowers will break the stalks on a hot day. Plant foxgloves only in shade. They are in no way suited to full or even partial sun in our hot climate. Even with shade protection and diligent watering, high heat may topple bloom stalks. You can try protecting foxgloves over the winter with lots of pine boughs placed over them after the ground has frozen, around Christmas. A mulch of leaves placed *around* them doesn't seem to improve their survival rate. A mulch of leaves placed *over* them will kill them.

Delphinium, perennial, size varies, sun: Here's trouble. Can't live with them. Can't live without them. If you have ever looked at a garden blessed with large, healthy, perennial delphiniums, you surely covet them for your own little plot. They are big, tall, richly colored, bold and yet fragile, stately, regal, breathtaking. Okay, I'm running out of adjectives. Delphiniums simply *make* the garden when they bloom from late June through the middle of July. Cut them back and a secondary flowering occurs, though it is very much a dim shadow of the glorious first bloom.

Here's the downside. Delphiniums will keel over in Midwestern wind, so they must be staked. Don't kid yourself into thinking you can get by without staking or with simple pea staking. These are big mamas and when they fall, they fall hard. Only good strong staking will do. A large cage is best. To make matters worse, their generous size is greatly reduced when the first flush of bloom ends and you trim them back to the side shoots. This leaves a gaping hole in the garden right where you've been focusing attention. Plenty of planning needs to go into how you will disguise this hole that occurs in midsummer. Consider planting your delphiniums behind plants like asters, chrysanthemums, or daylilies that reach their peak in late summer and autumn.

Thrilling as they are, I don't think delphiniums are worth the effort, but if, like sirens, they lure you on, at least do the best you can to keep them happy. All members of this genus like full sun, but in our hot climate you should try to place them where they get the protection of light or dappled shade during part of the afternoon. Too much shade will make the plants grow leggy. Delphiniums demand loose, deep, rich soil with excellent drainage. If you are attempting to garden without properly preparing your soil, don't expect to succeed with delphiniums. They must have moist soil but cannot stand in water, and only proper soil preparation and the addition of plenty of organic matter will give them that condition. When the first growth emerges in spring, thin each clump that is at least a year old to leave only the thickest five to seven stems. Feed them with a granular fertilizer at this point and with a liquid fertilizer when the first bloom is cut off.

Various pests and diseases threaten delphiniums. Slugs find them tasty. Powdery mildew is another hazard. Resign yourself to the reality of spraying regularly with fungicide or putting up with unsightly and damaging fungus. The usual advice is to avoid crowding the plants so that they have good air circulation around them, but in the heat and humidity of our summers, this precaution is unlikely to be effective. When the humidity is 95 percent and there isn't a breath of air stirring you could plant them alone in a square block and they'd probably still get powdery mildew.

If you're tempted by delphiniums take a look at Lynne Rathbone's excellent article "Growing Great English Delphiniums," published in *Fine Gardening* magazine (September–October 1994, 44–49).

Midsummer

Artemisia stelleriana (beach wormwood), perennial, height twelve
   inches, spreading habit, full sun: This beautiful perennial foliage
   plant bears soft, nappy, silver-white leaves similar to those of
   Centaurea cineraria, syn. *C. maritima* (dusty miller) on a low,
   spreading perennial plant. The sprays of yellow flowers in summer are more a distraction than a refinement. I cut them off as
   soon as they appear. *Artemisia stelleriana* glories in full hot sun
   and demands good drainage and dry weather. It won't do well
   in a clay soil. It is a master filler plant, closing up the gaps that
   can occur in a perennial planting. Get one. I love it. I'm betting
   you will, too.

Hosta (hosta or plantain lily), perennial, size varies, shade: Hostas
   come in a seemingly endless range of cultivars that offer great
   choice of size, form, texture, and leaf color. You could make a very
   lovely shade garden with a carefully chosen selection of these
   perennials and little else. Their big, broad leaves are their great
   feature, varying in color from a green so pale you might as well
   go ahead and call it yellow, through darker greens to a rich and
   frosty blue. Some are beautifully variegated. Although hostas
   send up pretty bloom stalks hung with large bells of white or pale
   lavender, the flowering is brief and definitely secondary to the
   foliage.

   In choosing hostas, pay attention to form. Most of them produce a tidy clump with leaves that curve back to earth neatly
   covering their feet, but some are vase shaped and will require an
   underplanting about their ankles. You also should take note of
   the mature size your chosen hosta can be expected to reach. It
   may grow slowly, reaching full size in four or five years or even
   longer. Once its mature size is realized, though, you don't want

to be moving it to a different location because it will (unless it is a miniature) be extremely heavy. Believe me, transplanting a mature hosta three feet across with roots firmly entrenched in fifteen inches of clay is no small task. The plant may easily weigh fifty pounds, and to dig it, lift it above ground, move it, and make a huge hole to accommodate it is serious work. A better approach is to put the hosta where it will stay and plant annuals or smaller perennials around it while it takes its time putting on girth.

Hostas are well-known plants for shade, but you often see them suggested for partial shade or even sun, too. Variegated hostas in particular may be suggested for sunny locations to maximize their variety of coloration. Beware this advice because our Midwestern sun is just too strong. Site hostas in moist, rich soil in full shade or in constant dappled shade. You can also place them where they receive direct sun only in early morning or very late afternoon. However, if you site them where they are caught out in the full glare of the midday or afternoon sun for even a short time, they will suffer in a heat wave. When temperatures top 100 degrees ugly brown patches will develop and remain for the rest of the season. Meanwhile, hostas in shady locations will show no sign of distress at all.

Among the hostas I've grown, I can especially recommend *H. sieboldiana* var. *elegans, H.* 'Krossa Regal,' and *H. sieboldiana* 'Frances Williams.' *H. sieboldiana* var. *elegans* is a behemoth beauty, a solid three feet high and as much or more across, with gorgeous frosty blue leaves that are rounded, thick, and textured. The first two or three years I had this plant I wondered what all the fuss was about. The darned thing looked green to me, not blue, and it certainly wasn't the flamboyant size I had been lead to expect. Then I read that *H. sieboldiana* var. *elegans* can take as long as seven years to reach maturity, and I settled back to watch patiently. After another couple of years, I saw that it was worth the wait. Both color and size developed over time. I have anchored each end of my shade border with one of these, and they are handsome indeed, creating the effect of a small shrub. The bloom is a solid cluster of white flowers, but it's held too close to the foliage to be showy.

H. 'Krossa Regal' is tall and distinguished by a decided vase shape that demands a low planting close about its feet. The color is a luminous blue gray that must be seen to be believed. The plant is about two feet tall, but the lavender blooms stand up high on four-foot stalks. This hosta is absolutely fearless in a heat wave. In the most scorching days of August it looks fresher than anything else in my garden.

H. 'Frances Williams' possesses leaves that are a slightly blue shade of green edged with a wide band of creamy yellow green that shimmers in dark shade.

If you plan to make a garden in shade, start with hostas and *Astilbe* (false spirea). They make ideal companions. Both are perfectly content in rich, moist shade, and the beautiful contrast of the wide, smooth hosta leaves with the lacy false spirea leaves is quite striking.

Gypsophila paniculata 'Bristol Fairy' (baby's breath), perennial, height thirty-six inches, spread thirty-six inches, sun: To see this perennial in full bloom is to want it—passionately. Baby's breath is that sweet, dainty, airy filler so commonly used in florist's bouquets. A multitude of tiny white blooms creates a three-foot cloud of white like a small blizzard. 'Bristol Fairy' continues this stunning effect for two or three weeks from late June through mid-July, its flowering coinciding with the bloom of *Lilium regale* (regal lily). A large bouquet of regal lilies and baby's breath will absolutely knock your socks off. I have taken this bouquet to a loved one in the hospital and it literally created a sensation. Total strangers stopped to ask about the flowers.

Gypsophila paniculata likes an alkaline soil, so add lime at planting time and be sure to provide good drainage to help prevent crown rot. The difficulty with baby's breath is that it is both so delicate and so large that it will flop horribly, and once flopped will be splattered with mud and ruined by the first hard rain. It's vital to take strong measures early. Instructions for making a girdling cage for baby's breath to grow in are provided in the staking section in chapter 6. It all sounds like a lot of fuss, but once the plant forms that huge cloud of airy white, you will forget all that. This is a truly splendid plant in full flower. I can hardly bear to mar it by picking any of the bloom, but it does make a superb filler in cut flower bouquets. It is also a very desirable dried flower. To dry it, simply cut and arrange it in your hand, then rubber-band or tie the stems together and hang it upside down in a dry, airy location until the stems turn brown. Do not attempt to dry it first and then arrange it, because once it is dry it shatters explosively.

After the first wave of bloom on the plant has faded, cut it back to a point where you see more flower buds forming and you will have a long-lasting secondary bloom. This second flowering, though inferior to the first wave, creates texture in the garden right through August and into September.

A baby's breath is not forever. This short-lived plant is likely to develop crown rot and die rapidly. When it happens, don't worry about it. Just replace your plant as quickly as possible. You don't want to be without this beauty.

Consolida (larkspur), annual, height twenty-four inches, spread twelve inches, sun: I always think of larkspurs as junior delphiniums, lesser in stature, but also free of many of the problems that come with the delphinium package. Larkspur blossoms are similar in form and color, but the plants haven't the dignified elegance of the more regal delphiniums.

Larkspur colors range from white and pink to shades of blue

and purple. The plants self-seed freely, scattering their offspring around your beds at random. Pulling up seedlings that spring up where you don't want them couldn't be easier. Larkspurs thrive in full sun, but will also tolerate light shade for at least part of the day. Their light and airy look is a great part of their charm, but the insubstantial quality of the whole plant means that massing larkspurs is not especially effective. These are casual flowers, not suited to the formal garden. I like them mingled loosely among my perennials. I think they are very good companions for tall bearded irises because they bloom after irises, from late in June through the end of July, filling in the bareness left in the absence of iris bloom.

Lilium (lily), bulb, size varies, sun or part shade: Something about lilies speaks of elegance, purity, and mystery. Their exquisite beauty is so desirable that you somehow feel they are unattainable. They must be terribly tricky and difficult to grow. Their aura daunts you. Or maybe it's the price. Lilies *are* pricey. No doubt about that. A typical tulip bulb costs around fifty cents. A lily can run ten times as much or even more. Never mind. It's worth the price of admission. If your budget is tight, add them gradually.

Lilies are organized into nine divisions and the range available is wide. How will you choose the ones you want? First, consider scent. Many lilies are very strongly and sweetly scented. If a heart beats in your breast you will certainly want some fragrant ones. This eliminates some of the modern hybrids from consideration. For good scent, try Oriental hybrids and trumpet lilies.

To further narrow your choice, consider height. The taller ones—those over about thirty inches—will need staking. The blooms are very large, and their weight might be too much for their stems even in a less windy part of the world. In our climate firm staking is an absolute necessity. If you resent the time spent staking or if accomplishing this sort of task on a timely basis is not your strong suit, avoid the taller lilies. On the other hand, if you want a vertical line, eschew the shorter ones.

The final point to consider is the appearance of the bloom: color and form. The colors include white, cream, pinks from very pale through deep rose, yellow, gold, peach, and orange. Many have edgings or markings of a second color, are freckled, or have yellow or pale green at the throat. On some flowers the stamens are particularly beautiful, but if you don't remove them, they will shed their pollen onto the petals and make an unsightly mess, so try to imagine how the flower will look after a haircut. Pay attention to whether the flowers face upward, downward, or outward. This will make a difference in how you wish to place them in your garden. Obviously the downward-facing blooms are less showy, though they may be quite beautiful cut and placed in a vase at eye level.

Oriental hybrids have rather flat blooms with petals that are curved backward, sometimes tightly, at the tips. Petals may be wide or narrow, smooth or textured. They may ruffle a bit at the edges or twist slightly as they curve backward. The trumpet lilies, though suggested in some reference sources for zones 4–8, may be best grown in areas with warmer winters. If you like the trumpet shape, try *L. regale.* The Asiatic hybrids lack scent, but they do offer plenty of bloom and are the earliest bloomers. The petals are smooth and most have upward-facing flowers. They also thrive in our tough climate and reproduce themselves well.

The commonest garden lily of them all, *L. lancifolium,* syn. *L. tigrinum,* the tiger lily, is very easy to grow and will spread by bulbil. Bulbils are those little black beads that grow up and down the stems at the base of each leaf. Lilies can be propagated by seed, by bulbil, or by separating the bulb into scales and planting them. In the case of tiger lilies, the plants propagate themselves quite freely from the bulbils. When you don't want any more tiger lilies, just start pulling up the seedlings.

Tiger lilies thrive in heat, blooming in August with several flowers on each three-to-five-foot stem. Even the taller ones seldom need staking. Tiger lilies are known to be carriers of lily mosaic virus, and garden books routinely advise against planting them near other kinds of lilies to avoid the spread of this disease. However, if you think you can be satisfied with just one kind of lily and have a taste for flowers in the hot color range, these orange beauties may be just right for you. Their propensity for self-propagation makes them an economical choice. Unfortunately, they have no scent.

L. regale, the regal lily, has a tall stalk that will certainly require staking. Catalogs suggest that it will grow four or five feet tall, but mine routinely reached six feet and occasionally topped out at the eaves of my ranch-style home. The mid-July blooms have the classic white trumpet appearance of florists' Easter lilies. The outsides are pinkish purple to varying extent. This coloration was very faint in my garden and may be reduced by the heat of our climate. Each stem carries several blossoms, making quite a stunning display when at peak bloom. Regal lilies have a potent sweet scent that is especially strong in the evening. When cut, one stem can scent an entire house.

L. 'Casa Blanca' is a stately Oriental hybrid. As with others of this type, plant it in dappled shade or where it is protected from afternoon sun because it suffers when temperatures rise above 90 degrees. In 1995 when two heat waves over 100 degrees were blasting my garden, the 'Casa Blanca' plants that I had sited in full sun developed brown patches on both leaf and petal. If you have been equally foolish in site selection, cut the flower stems as the lower flowers begin to open and take them indoors. They will open and stay fresh in a vase over a remarkably long time. One stem makes a truly majestic bouquet. The flowers are extravagantly large and so shockingly pure white that you need to be careful where you place them because so many other flowers will be dingy in their company. Bloom begins late in July. The wonderful scent reminds me of vanilla.

L. 'Bonnie,' an Asiatic hybrid, is short, about two feet tall, with several pale pink, upward-facing flowers that bloom from the end of June through mid-July. Though unscented, 'Bonnie' does reproduce itself freely and has made a nice show reliably for something like twelve years in my garden. In that time, I have dug and given away excess bulbs twice.

L. 'Pink Virtuoso' is an Oriental hybrid with big white flowers blushed two tones of pink (dark and darker) down the center of each petal and liberally sprinkled with dark rose spots. This lily blooms from late July through mid-August. In our climate it is likely to be damaged in full sun and unlikely to return year after year.

Lilies are perennials. Give them a nice, deep, rich soil with excellent drainage in dappled shade or morning sun with afternoon sun protection. Full sun is fine for tiger lilies, Asiatic lilies, and regal lilies. Fertilize them with a granular fertilizer once a year, in spring when the leaves first emerge from the ground. If you cut them for bouquets, don't take more than a third of the stem because the remaining foliage must nourish the bulb.

Astilbe (false spirea), perennial, size varies, shade: Although these perennials are sometimes suggested for full sun, don't even think about it. These are clearly shade plants in our climate because they need plenty of moisture. Dig in a lot of compost and while you're at it throw in some manure, because *Astilbe* like a very rich soil. They are known as gross feeders, meaning they use up the good stuff in the soil faster than other plants. I scratch in extra manure and compost around them in the spring and give them a second helping after they bloom. They thrive on this treatment. If you don't have the time to enrich your soil with plenty of humus, don't even bother with *Astilbe*. They won't thrive for you.

The fresh and attractive foliage is every bit as good a reason to grow false spirea as the flower. The dark green leaves are deeply cut and reminiscent of ferns. There is a stiff uprightness about the foliage that gives the plants a shrubby presence in the garden in spite of the delicacy of the leaves. A myriad of tiny flowers form the inflorescence, often in the form of an inverted cone that presents a feathery look. This unusual bloom shape adds great interest. Flower colors are white and various shades of pink and purple.

Numerous varieties and cultivars exist, so shop around for those that suit you in size and color. *A. chinensis* var. *pumila* makes a great ground cover because it spreads rapidly to form a dense mass, but not so quickly as to be a nuisance. (You may have to jump back after planting it, but you won't have to run for the ax.) The flowers are lavender pink and less feathery than those of other varieties. The long flowering period begins in mid-July, peaks about the first of August, and ends two weeks later.

A. 'Sprite' is a bit taller (about a foot high and the same across). Its loosely branched pale pink flower heads arch gracefully for a sweetly delicate appearance. Flowering occurs the last two weeks in July.

A. 'Brautschleier,' syn. *A.* 'Bridal Veil' is about two feet high with blooms held another six inches above the plant. The white flowers, in the classic plume form, occur from the last week in June through the middle of July, when seed heads begin to form and the bloom heads turn ecru. You can leave them on for lasting interest and—if you're lucky—even the occasional false spirea from seed.

A. chinensis var. *taquetii* 'Superba' is about four feet high when in bloom and two feet across. The blooms are more tightly placed and do not form the feathery cone of many other *Astilbe*. The pink-purple flowers occur from mid-July into August.

Coreopsis verticillata 'Moonbeam' (threadleaf tickseed), perennial, height ten–twelve inches, spreading habit, sun: The quantity of bloom on this drought-tolerant, carefree gem is quite extraordinary in the world of perennial plants. As a result, it's often used by landscapers to provide a long season of color. You might find it looking stiff and uncomfortable in a mulch of wood chips in the green space around some chain restaurant. To my eye, this plant looks far happier and more graceful at the front of a perennial border where it obligingly weaves in among its neighbors.

Coreopsis verticillata 'Moonbeam' is low-growing, spreading ever wider. It will gradually fill whatever space you allow it, but is readily pulled or dug out if it creeps in where it isn't wanted, so it poses no threat to neighboring perennials. Bits you dig up can be easily moved to fill other spots. The leaves are threadlike. The blooms, produced in showers from late June through September, are small, lemon yellow, and rayed like daisies. Blossoming will lag somewhere in the middle of the bloom season, about mid-August. Some gardeners advise shearing the plant back at this point to promote additional bloom. I find that if I just wait a couple of weeks bloom returns anyway and I haven't sacrificed the plant's shape. Shearing actually removes large numbers of flower buds. Don't take my word on this, though. Shear back half your plants and leave the rest, then stand back and decide what works best in your own garden.

Rudbeckia fulgida var. *sullivantii* 'Goldsturm' (black-eyed Susan), perennial, height twenty inches, spreading habit, sun: This is a workhorse perennial. It blooms from the first of July through late September, most of this period covering itself in blossoms. It makes a nice sturdy bush of a plant that is oblivious to the fierce winds of our region. The stiff stems stand up beautifully and look good even in winter if you forgo cutting the bloom stalks down in fall. The seed heads are a nice presence in the garden in frost and snow.

'Goldsturm' spreads continuously, but doesn't invade and choke its neighbors when you turn your back for a few minutes. It isn't one of those dreaded plants to which the term *vigorous* is so deceptively applied in catalogs. (If crabgrass were offered in nursery catalogs, it would be called "vigorous," as if that were an accolade.) You can divide black-eyed Susans frequently to increase your stock or just dig the plants up every three or four years and replant only a small part if you prefer to keep them contained.

This plant also goes to seed fairly prolifically, and unless you are diligent about removing seedlings, your garden will soon be a sea of gold. Removal of seedlings is quite easy while they are small. Just pay attention to the foliage so you can pick out the 'Goldsturm' seedlings, then pull them by hand as you see them in spring. If you let them grow on a bit, you'll have to get out a hoe to dig them out. To avoid the problem of excess seedlings altogether, you can simply deadhead the flowers as they fade. Of course, this means forgoing the ornamental seed heads in your winter garden.

Zinnia, annual, size varies, sun: Zinnias possess truly uninspiring foliage. Their pallid green leaves of no particular texture or ornamental shape can, however, be excused for the wealth of bloom they support. Zinnias are annuals that begin blooming in late June or early July and keep it up nearly until frost. They come in a range of colors from white, yellow, and orange to varying shades of pink and vivid reds and purples. Most commonly seen in gardens are the mixed colors sold everywhere in the spring. These are bright and cheerful, but if you have a color scheme and aim to do something artistic in your garden, don't expect to find single color six-packs at the nursery. Mix and match or grow your own from seed. You can still buy single colors of some varieties if you order from seed catalogs, though the sad trend seems to be toward nothing but mixes.

You can plant big beds of zinnias for a solid color display from midsummer on. This is certainly a common use of them. I think, though, that they are at their best sprinkled into a perennial border where surrounding plants with more intriguing foliage keep you from noticing the zinnias' weakness in this area. Zinnias are very likely to get a disfiguring powdery mildew in late summer. It strikes me that the more you plant of them in close proximity the more they are likely to be attacked and devastated, so scattering them among your perennials is a good idea from that viewpoint, too. You can spray them to control powdery mildew, but if the disease occurs very late in the summer when flowering is beginning to diminish, you may want to simply pull up the plants, leaving more space for late bloomers. Late season asters, chrysanthemums, *Boltonia asteroides,* and butterfly bushes are taking center stage, so the loss of a few zinnias is no great tragedy.

Zinnias are extremely easy to grow from seed and will germinate in just a few days. You can expect a high percentage of successful germination, so you will probably get more plants than you need from just one seed packet. Give your extras to friends. Plant zinnias in full sun. They are not at all fussy about richness of soil and take only an average amount of water. Because of their susceptibility to powdery mildew, try to water them at the base, not on the leaves.

Petunia, annual, size varies, sun: Petunias thrive in summer heat and fierce sunlight. Their low mounded form makes them ideal for edging borders. They also look great billowing out of pots. Started indoors and set out in mid-May, petunias begin blooming six weeks later and don't quit until frost. Their popularity means they are widely available in a variety of colors from white and yellow to pink, lavender, and purple.

Tagetes (marigold), annual, size varies, sun: Marigolds are very popular annuals, judging by the abundance of six-packs you see in
almost every garden shop in spring. They bloom heavily for a
very long time, from about the first of July through frost. Most
commonly found in the brashest orange, they also come in lemony yellow and clear golds. They've even been bred in a white
form. Although marigolds last all right in water, they don't make
good cut flowers because they are so closely branched that picking one flower means sacrificing oncoming bloom from the buds
that come along with it.

I'm partial to the smaller, single-blossomed marigolds. They
are a foot high or less and have flowers only an inch or so across.
Look for the ones in the Gem Series or Disco Series. If you choose
a shade of yellow or orange that appeals to you, a few small patches of these can add dash to the overall look of your garden. I like
the lemon-yellow ones because they suit my favorite color
scheme, but if you go in for a hot color scheme, the orange marigolds should fit in nicely.

The dark ferny foliage of marigolds has a pungent odor when
bruised. Some people find this smell offensive, others enjoy it. If
it's not to your taste, site marigolds where you won't be constantly brushing up against them.

Nicotiana (tobacco plant), size varies, sun to light shade: For heady,
powerful scent that permeates a wide area, you can't beat *Nicotiana alata,* syn. *N. affinis* (flowering tobacco). It is in a class with
roses on this score. I'm not talking about the modern hybrids that
make tidy little clumps good for edging and prolific bloom. For
fragrance go straight for the original. *N. alata* is a big, frowzy
plant that will sprawl about your garden taking up far more space
than you had intended and failing to show the slightest restraint.
You will want to stake it somehow, but the stems are so brittle

and the leaves so soft that propping efforts won't be successful. By the end of June, just before *N. alata* begins blooming, you will have begun to wonder why you put the darned thing out there in the first place.

Ah, but then the flowers begin. They are like white trumpets flaring into a star at the tip. There whiteness is luminous, making the flowers seem to float above the bed, particularly at night when they emerge startlingly clear from the dusk. This is happy timing, as they also release their staggering perfume in the evening. Walk out after dinner to let it waft over you in sweet waves. The flowering and scent are continuous until frost. This steady display makes *N. alata* a good choice for planting in number to form one strong element of a garden. Its blowzy habit makes it less than desirable for planting in great masses, but it doesn't take masses to create an effect. Half a dozen plants, placed in pairs at intervals along a border, will sweep the area with scent and provide that nice unifying sense of repetition. *N. alata* is a short-lived perennial, best treated as an annual.

Another heavily scented flowering tobacco is *N. sylvestris,* a magnificent thing that makes a shoulder-high plant topped with clusters of pendant white flowers from late summer into fall. Though it blooms for a shorter time, the effect is big and bold. Put a single plant near a gate as a specimen or create the feeling of columns in a border by planting several spaced along both sides of a path with a froth of lower plants at their feet.

If you absolutely insist on something a bit tidier, try *N.* 'Lime Green.' It forms neat little clumps about one foot high and two feet across with pale sulfur yellow flowers all summer. Though it is lovely, it is unscented.

I have admired *N. langsdorfii* in photos, but in my garden the plants were spindly and the flowers seemed to fall off almost before they opened. It is apparently quite variable in height, being described as three to five feet tall. Mine were at the shorter end. The flowers are a pale green, slightly olive, dangling, and less flared at the tips than other types, so they'll look unusual in your garden. Go ahead and try them. Perhaps they will fare better for you. To make a show, you probably need several planted together about one foot apart.

Borago officinalis (borage), annual, height twenty-four to thirty-six inches, spread twelve inches, sun to part shade: Borage is a very nice annual if you like a cottage garden look. It doesn't transplant well, so start it from seed directly in the garden where you want it to grow. You will need to plant it only once, as it seeds itself very freely, and here's where that cottage garden feeling comes into play. Let the plants flourish where the seeds fall for a casual, unplanned look. The plants are a bit lank and lazy and will flop and spill over border edges, giving you a look of happy abundance from late summer on. Borage flowers over a long season from late June through the end of September.

The leaves, stems, and buds are heavily textured, hairy, and a bit prickly, producing an overall misty look. Foliage color is soft green with a blue cast to it. The star-shaped flowers are only one-half to three-quarters inch across, but they are a very intense sapphire blue with a black center. Although the plant is theoretically three feet tall, its floppy habit often means that it is more like two feet off the ground.

Lobularia maritima, syn. *Alyssum maritimum* (sweet alyssum), annual, height four–five inches, spread twelve inches, sun: I read once, I can't recall where, a pooh-poohing of sweet alyssum that suggested it was trite and commonplace and that only the least imaginative gardener would use it. This sweeping condemnation seems to me wildly off-base. Most cultivars of sweet alyssum cover themselves so densely in tiny white flowers that the leaves are all but invisible. The whiteness of the flowers is as pure and snowy as anything you will see anywhere in nature. Sweet alyssum makes this floral offering for an astonishingly long period, from the last week in June through the third week in October. If this were not enough, it is lavishly fragrant. Though the plant is a ground hugger, the scent is very noticeable as you stroll through the garden on a warm day, your nose never closer than five feet away. The fragrance reminds me strongly of honey and I consider it as sweet and fine as that of roses.

Plant sweet alyssum from seed or buy seedlings in the six-packs widely available in nurseries in spring. For about a month after you set them out, they are so insignificant that you may wonder why you bothered with them, but be patient. They soon form lovely floral pools spilling over border edges or down the sides of raised beds. They make very nice pot plants set about the base of some larger, more upright specimen.

Anethum graveolens (dill), annual, size varies, sun: Dill, of course, is an herb. The threadlike leaves can be chopped up to season an egg salad sandwich or a grilled salmon steak. The seeds have their culinary uses, too, so this plant is usually relegated to the herb garden. Its flowers, though, if you take a minute to notice, are quite lovely—airy and graceful and a wonderful acid yellow. The plant is tall but insubstantial with feathery foliage that seems to float weightlessly in the garden. Plants vary considerably in height from about twenty-four to about thirty-six inches. A three-foot-tall plant takes up almost no width, however, so you can toss a few seeds in among perennials.

Dill is a very easy plant that takes no care at all. Site it in full sun. It's an annual that flowers for a few weeks starting in mid-July. The blooms make terrific cut flowers, but leave a few on the plant to form seed. Scatter the seed where you want the plants to grow in next year's garden. If you are lucky, in mid- to late summer you'll notice striped caterpillars on the plants. Allow them to eat their fill and then watch for the swallowtail butterflies to appear. This magical event adds great charm to a garden. Share it with a child. When the caterpillars are through with the dill, just pull it up and toss it on the compost pile.

Echinops ritro (small globe thistle), perennial, height forty-eight inches, spread twenty-four inches, sun: Small globe thistle has a hard edge to it that makes a nifty contrast to all the soft stuff in your border. Its stiffly upright form has a primeval feel. You can imagine *Echinops ritro* in bloom when dinosaurs roamed the Midwest. Though relatively tall, this perennial never needs staking and could in fact be used among floppy plants to help hold them up. Its bloom, from mid-July through the first week in August, is as stiff and prickly as the plant itself. The globe-shaped thistle is about the size of a marshmallow and a color usually described as steely blue, though I think it is too attractive a shade to be so harshly labeled. This is one of those wonderful garden flowers that is truly blue and not the lavender, purple, or violet often called blue in garden literature.

E. *ritro* is a definite conversation starter. Visitors are likely to come to a full, screeching halt in front of it and demand to know what it is. Probably they are startled to see in cultivation something that looks so much like the thistle that is considered a noxious weed by farmers and is actually illegal to have growing on your property in my state. There's nothing weedy about E. *ritro*. Though it will self-sow if you leave the blooms to ripen and form seed, the seedlings are not numerous and are easily pulled. It's a good idea to allow seed to form though, because the ripening seed heads hold the bloom form and some of its color for several weeks, giving the plant at least a semblance of extended bloom. You can dry the flowers for use in wreaths or arrangements, but the trick is to take the flowers just *before* they reach full bloom.

My small globe thistle is planted behind a daylily that has the sunset colors of deep rose layered over apricot (*Hemerocallis* 'Bowl of Roses'). The spiky blooms and angular form of small globe thistle make it the perfect backdrop for the straplike foliage and fat, thick blooms of this daylily. I have only one small globe thistle, but I have seen this plant used at intervals throughout a long border to provide the pleasant unity of spaced repetition, like columns on a grand porch.

E. ritro is very reliable, performing year after year. It increases in size slowly so that it takes quite a while to get too big for its britches. Part of its reliability, unfortunately, is that in my garden I can count on its being attacked by aphids nearly every spring about late May. The good news is that these pests can be easily controlled.

Hemerocallis (daylily), perennial, size varies, sun: If you think you don't like these perennials, you probably don't really know them. Neophyte gardeners often believe that all daylilies are orange, and when it comes to orange daylilies, familiarity breeds contempt. These are the old-fashioned flowers that bloom in ditches and on old farm sites. They bore you silly. I'm talking here about something else again. Modern hybridizers have created a fabulous range of daylilies that includes colors as pale as a frosty yellow that comes very close to white, as vivid as dark reds and purples, as elusive as deep rose layered over apricot. Blooms are made up of wide and heavy petals or of long, thin, and curling ones. They are crimped at their edges or sprinkled with stardust or built around a brilliant green heart. The variety is thrilling. The colors are flashy in the garden. Best of all, these plants bloom well and thrive in the worst heat of summer when much of the rest of the garden is out of flower, wilted, or half dead.

A word of caution about daylilies: the blooms are varied, but the foliage is not. The green straplike leaves are all but identical from one cultivar to the next. Dwarf plants make smaller clumps and perhaps thinner leaves, but the essential character of the foliage does not vary. If you plant a great many of them, the repetition may go unnoticed while the plants bloom, but it will be a great screaming bore when they are not in flower. Furthermore, the leaves rise in an arching fountain that takes up quite a lot of space by midsummer. Unless you plan carefully, this can leave quite a few gaping holes in your spring garden.

I like to plant tall bearded irises among my daylilies. When the daylily plants are small in spring, the irises hold sway with their lovely orchidlike flowers and great swirls of silvery green leaf. By mid- to late summer, the iris foliage is likely to be unattractive. No problem. The daylilies hide it. The irises don't seem to suffer from being slightly shaded for part of the summer. You could also plant bulbs among your daylilies to provide spring bloom because they go dormant by the time the daylilies reach full size.

By the way, though all *Hemerocallis* are called daylilies, they are decidedly not lilies. Lilies are in the genus *Lilium* and are something else entirely. The daylily is a perennial plant with thick roots, numerous leaves emerging from the ground, and several stems of flower buds. Each flower lasts only one day. The lily, on the other hand, is a bulb made up of thick scales. It is planted deeply and produces one stem of flowers with numerous leaves up and down the stem. Each lily flower lasts a few days to two weeks. The only real similarity between lilies and daylilies is in the shape of the bloom.

Each daylily stem produces many flower buds that mature and bloom successively. Though each blossom lasts only one day, there are so many of them that an individual plant blooms over several weeks. The daylily is generally not used as a cut flower because the blossom will last only a few hours and you will have sacrificed the garden bloom of all of the buds picked with that stem.

Most daylilies open in the morning, last through the day, and close in the evening. Because their flowers fade as the day

progresses, especially in extreme heat and brilliant sun, particularly if the flowers are in the red-purple range, they are at their
best in the morning. If you do most of your gardening in the
evening, look for hybrids that open in the afternoon and close
the following morning. This will allow you to enjoy your daylilies at their best.

Though not generally thought of as fragrant flowers, many daylilies have a very pleasing, sweet fragrance. This is a characteristic
to watch for in selecting daylilies for your garden. Like many other flowers, they are most fragrant in the evening, so selecting for
scent is particularly important if you are an after-work gardener.

Often *Hemerocallis* producers' catalogs will picture only a few
of their newest offerings. Be warned that these recent introductions are also the most expensive. The longer a daylily is around,
the lower the price falls. Some lovely cultivars have been on the
market long enough that their prices are quite reasonable. On the
other hand, spanking new offerings—so beautiful they make you
pant—are often wildly expensive. Get the most for your garden
buck by waiting a bit till the price goes down to acquire those
lovelies. Meanwhile, purchase the tried and true and economical oldies. I confess that in 1988 I violated my own advice by paying the shocking price of $17.75 for a tempting daylily called
H. 'Bowl of Roses.' The photo showed a flower of such rich, sunset colors that I could not bear to pass it up. By the second year,
it was a large plant with plenty of big beautiful blooms. I thought,
and still do, that it lived up completely to that catalog photo and
description. Though I have never regretted purchasing it, six
years later 'Bowl of Roses' could be had for just $10.50. By com-
parison, lovely older cultivars like *H.* 'Daydream Believer,' *H.*
'Little Fat Dazzler,' and *H.* 'Prairie Blue Eyes' can be had for $5.00
or $6.00.

Though a few daylilies increase slowly, most become larger at
a moderately rapid rate and are relatively easy to dig and divide.

A three- or four-year-old clump can readily be turned into three to five smaller plants that will provide bloom the following year.

You often read in garden books that daylilies are carefree, pest free, and need never be watered. This is a bit of an exaggeration. While daylilies are certainly very tough plants, they are not completely without problems. Although they survive times of drought without water, they definitely bloom best if you water them regularly as you do other perennials. In protracted extreme heat (above 100 degrees), their leaves will scorch somewhat. Following bloom, some of the leaves will die back but will be replaced shortly by fresh new growth. Just pull off and discard the dead leaves.

In some seasons daylilies will form buds nicely but drop many of them before they can bloom. This seems to be the unavoidable result of certain weather conditions. Some years this problem is severe, other times it is negligible.

Your daylilies may also suffer from some pests. Mine are regularly assaulted by tarnished plant bugs (*Lygus lineolaris*). These annoying insects cause buds to shrivel. They dart to the back of a bud or leaf or simply fly away when you try to hand pick them. Although you can control them by spraying with malathion, the spray also is extremely deadly to bees. It's better to simply live with them and the damage they cause. Just turn a blind eye to the little devils. The overall appearance of your plant won't be noticeably affected, and daylilies are such generous bloomers that you can afford to sacrifice a bit for the safety of the bees.

If you plant a new daylily only to have it refuse to bloom, check to see whether it is planted too deeply. Sometimes they sink in soft prepared soil and then refuse to blossom. The top of the root structure should be only about a half inch below the ground's surface.

Thalictrum rochebrunianum 'Lavender Mist' (meadow rue), perennial, height five feet, spread two feet, part shade: This beautiful cultivar of *Thalictrum* is one of those plants whose dimensions in no way indicate its true form. Although it is indeed tall, most of its foliage grows near the ground. The long stems are thick and stout and may need no staking because they support only airy clouds of tiny flowers. As big as this perennial is, it seems light and insubstantial.

You could put one of these smack in front of the border to interrupt the monotony of plants ranked strictly by height. You could throw in four or five scattered along the length of a large border to give vertical line and unity. Or cluster several together for a cool haze of bloom.

'Lavender Mist' likes to grow in a lightly shaded area in moist soil. Flowering starts in mid-July and continues for several weeks before seed forms, which gives the plant interest through most of September.

Aster x *frikartii* 'Mönch,' perennial, height twenty-four to forty inches, spread twenty-four to thirty inches, sun: If you don't already possess this plant (unfortunately not hardy in zone 4), hurry to the nearest nursery to correct this oversight as soon as possible. The color of the blooms alone makes this perennial worth having. Its rayed flowers, roughly two inches across, are a heavenly pale blue that is just faintly lavender. In a world where every dull lavender or purple plant is described as blue, this one truly is. 'Mönch' is also an abundant bloomer. As if this weren't enough, the length of bloom, from mid-July through at least the end of September, is extraordinary. Without pea staking the plant will flop forward, so that the overall clump is lower than described in some garden books. It is not, however, lank, and still looks very solid and full. It's gorgeous draped over the front edge of a raised bed. I have been told by a professional that 'Mönch' can be difficult to establish, but I haven't found it so. If the first plant you try doesn't succeed, try again. And again, if necessary.

When you get a clump going you'll find the show justifies the trouble.

Salvia farinacea 'Victoria' (mealycup sage), annual, height eighteen–thirty inches, spread fourteen inches, sun: This is the first annual blue *Salvia* cultivar that I recall seeing widely offered. Other cultivars have followed it, but I don't think any of them holds a candle to this one. The color is a very pure and piercing blue violet that looks like a rich velvet. The plant is small and compact, unlike some other annual types of sage that are on the rangy side. The flowers are small and spaced along a stalk, creating an overall bloom look that is both nicely textured and vertical. The seed heads are only slightly less blue—like the softly faded upholstery on your favorite chair. You can deadhead mealycup sage early on to keep it blooming. When weather turns cold enough to stop oncoming bloom, allow the seed heads to form, which gives the appearance of extended bloom. The plant will tend to flop over toward the light. I do realize that this should be a fault, but it somehow makes 'Victoria' more compatible for mixing with perennials.

Four plants of *Salvia farinacea* 'Victoria' set out in a diamond shape will make a nice splash of dark blue from mid-July until frost—three solid months, at least. Come August when they are looking absolutely smashing, I guarantee you will wish you had planted more.

Tanacetum parthenium, syn. *Chrysanthemum parthenium* (feverfew), short-lived perennial, height eighteen inches, spread twelve inches, sun or part shade: *Tanacetum parthenium* is a very nice, unassuming little plant that seems able to grow in almost any situation. In my garden it prospers in moist shade, but seems equally happy growing among the bricks of my patio in the full glare of the sun. Feverfew is a low-growing plant with a nice splash of white bloom like a bouquet of small daisies just right to hold in one hand. Flowering doesn't start until late June or mid-July, but continues without a breather until frost. The leaves are dark and lacy and pungently scented.

Although it is a hardy perennial, feverfew is short-lived. Fortunately, though, it will seed itself freely, so that you need plant it only once to enjoy it for many years. Scatter the seed directly in the garden, then pull any that fall where your eye tells you they don't belong. The result is casual and very sweet.

Late Summer

Ocimum basilicum 'Dark Opal' (basil), annual, height fifteen–eighteen inches, spread twelve inches, sun: *Ocimum basilicum* 'Dark Opal' makes attractive foliage for the flower garden. Its dark purple leaves appear spectacular contrasted with the green and gray of other foliage types and look especially beautiful with flowers in the pink range. As an added bonus, you'll be able to harvest some of the leaves for culinary flavoring. Basil strongly dislikes being transplanted, so it's far easier to start it from seed directly in the garden than to buy small sets. Basil is exceptionally tender and susceptible to cold. Don't plant it early, because a late cold snap is very likely to cut its life short. Your plant will show damage from which it may not recover even if temperatures do not drop all the way to freezing.

Perovskia atriplicifolia (Russian sage), perennial, height forty-eight inches, spread forty-eight inches, sun: A friend in the nursery trade says Russian sage can be a tough sell because a young plant looks like a stick in a pot. However unprepossessing it may look at this stage, buy one and plant it in a sunny spot. By the end of the second summer you will be wondering how you lived without it. Russian sage has a big bushy form and airy look that remind me of baby's breath. Though reference books suggest it is not hardy in zone 4, friends who garden north of Minneapolis say they have had good luck getting it through the winter with some shelter.

The stems and narrow toothed leaves are a woolly gray green that is more gray than green. The blooms from late July into September are a grayish blue and are followed for another month by seed pods of very much the same color. The overall effect is soft and hazy in spite of the rigidity of the stems.

P. atriplicifolia tends to lean heavily toward the sun unless you get one of the cultivars that stands more upright, such as 'Longin' or 'Filagran.' 'Longin' is wider and 'Filagran' has more finely cut leaves. I have the plain old species plant *P. atriplicifolia,* an incorrigible flopper. I am very fond of it and think that for some purposes, its arching flop is ideal. I also grow 'Filagran' for its graceful upright habit. It is beautiful with *Hemerocallis* 'Little Grapette,' whose raspberry red blooms are enhanced by association with the soft colors of the Russian sage.

Russian sage likes a sunny position and good drainage. Drought won't faze it, but soggy ground certainly will. If you have difficulty getting it going, improve the drainage of your soil and try again. Don't cut it down in fall, but wait until spring, about six weeks before the frost-free date, when you should prune it hard, cutting it back to just a foot or so off the ground. Its is a pleasant experience, because the stems and foliage have a pungent scent when bruised or cut. The plant soon puts on new foliage to make a nice bushy shape.

Thymophylla tenuiloba, syn. *Dyssodia tenuiloba* (Dahlberg daisy or golden fleece), annual, height six–eight inches, spread six inches, sun: This pleasing annual has half-inch daisylike flowers of clear yellow gold and delicate ferny foliage that delivers a strong, pungent, and delightful fragrance when crushed. As sweet and fragile as it looks, the Dahlberg daisy is a tough little customer that flourishes in strong sunlight or a bit of shade. I enjoy it mixed with other annuals in the containers on my brick patio. Plants from past summers have gone to seed in the brick, where they prosper with no care and very little moisture. You can buy the plants already in flower and set them out in May for continuous bloom through September. Seedlings from these parent plants will start blooming in July the following year.

Buddleia davidii (butterfly bush), shrub, size varies, sun: In milder climates, *Buddleia davidii* live through winter to form sizable shrubs, but in zone 5 they die back severely and must grow from nearly the ground up each season. They are not hardy in zone 4. Leave all of their growth on them until early spring, about four to six weeks before the frost-free date. Then prune them back hard to eight or twelve inches above ground level. They are slow to get started in spring, but will eventually put on growth and reach a height of four to seven feet by late in the season. Because of their slow start, you might want to plant bulbs at their feet to provide some spring show. Small flowers are borne in clusters like tapered bottle brushes from the first of August through frost— about ten weeks. Their sweet scent is unlike anything else in the garden. Butterflies find them irresistible and this, along with their substantial size, is a great part of their appeal. *B. davidii* 'Lochinch' has silvery gray leaves and lavender-blue flowers. Other butterfly bushes have dark green leaves and blooms in shades of purple and pink. This plant requires a site in full sun and will languish without it.

Calamintha (calamint), perennial, size varies, sun: Sweetly minty when you brush past it, covered in tiny flowers from late July until frost, absolutely pest-free, *Calamintha nepeta* (lesser calamint) is one terrific perennial. It forms a remarkably tidy clump, like a tiny

Mertensia pulmonarioides, syn. *M. virginica* (Virginia bluebells; garden of Aileen Rodgers and Jack Rodgers).

Right: Baptisia australis (blue wild indigo, false indigo, or plains false indigo).

Below: Artemisia stelleriana 'Silver Brocade' (beach wormwood).

Narcissus 'Thalia' (daffodil) with red tulips.

Below: Spiky *Calamintha nepeta* (lesser calamint) with *Geranium sanguineum* var. *striatum,* syn. *G. sanguineum* var. *lancastriense.*

Lamium maculatum 'Pink Pewter' (spotted deadnettle).

Secret garden with *Iris* 'Caesar's Brother' (Siberian iris) in foreground, *Iris* 'White Swirl' (Siberian iris) in background (photo by James L. McKee).

Right: Coreopsis verticillata 'Moonbeam' (threadleaf tickseed).

Dicentra spectabilis (bleeding heart) at left. At right a yellow *Epimedium* (barrenwort; garden of Aileen Rodgers and Jack Rodgers).

Cleome (spider flower) with *Daphne* x *burkwoodii* 'Carol Mackie' and *Athyrium niponicum* (Japanese painted fern; photo by James L. McKee).

shrub, with stiff and brittle stems. The flowers make pretty filler for the smallest bouquets and can easily be snapped off rather than cut. The overall appearance is sweet, delicate, and graceful. This is an exceptionally fine plant if you strive for a soft romantic look. Bees and wasps find it irresistible. I enjoy the busy hum this adds to the garden.

C. nepeta blooms from the end of July through the third week in October. The flowers are generally described as light blue, but in Midwestern heat they are more likely to be white with only the slightest whiff of blue about them. Then autumn arrives and the cool night air does seem to bring out their color. The plant is about twenty inches high by thirty inches wide.

C. grandiflora 'Variegata' is another very good perennial of the same family. It forms a lower clump (fifteen inches high by eighteen inches wide) and adds sparkle to the front of the border with its small, variegated leaves and purple-pink blooms. Flowering begins in mid-May and runs into early September. Shear the plant back and it may give you some bonus late bloom, too. During a late May tour of my garden, this plant attracted considerable notice.

Site *Calamintha* in full sun or a very little shade. Both kinds are oblivious to heat and dry conditions.

Cleome (spider flower), annual, height sixty inches, spread thirty-six inches, sun to part shade: If you want to make a statement in your garden, plant a few *Cleome*. People will sit up and take notice. These bold annuals start easily from seed the size of a fleck of pepper, growing by late summer into plants as big as you are. The flowers are softball-size exotic clusters of white or shades of rose and purple. These are my husband's favorite flowers, but they aren't to everyone's taste. A friend says they look like they're from outer space and I don't think she means it as a compliment.

Plant the seed directly in the garden, because seedlings do not transplant well. In late summer, the flowers will go to seed, making plenty for future use. Let the seed drop in place to start next year's crop or harvest it and scatter it where you like—no need to scratch the soil or cover the seed. These things are self-starters. Spider flowers positively glory in direct sun and heat, but will also do well in moderate shade. Bloom starts the end of July and continues without hesitation until the first hint of frost.

Fall

Boltonia asteroides 'Snowbank,' perennial, height forty-eight inches, spread twenty-four inches, sun: Like asters, perennial *Boltonia asteroides* blooms only in the late summer and fall, but takes up a sizable space throughout the season. Unlike asters, it has a relatively short bloom period, flowering for most of September but in really blazing full bloom for perhaps just two weeks. Is it worth it? It's a matter of taste, but you might prefer to forgo it if your garden is small.

'Snowbank' increases easily by division, and three plants will make a good showy grouping. The stems are very stiff and strong, so the plant needs no staking even in the windy Midwest. The snowy white rayed flowers are an inch wide or a bit less. They are extremely profuse, blooming all together in a great burst that makes a cloud of white. Bees, butterflies, and other insects are drawn to *Boltonia asteroides,* so no small part of the plant's show is the buzz of activity around it.

Anemone tomentosa 'Robustissima,' syn. *A. vitifolia* 'Robustissima' (grape-leaf anemone), perennial, height thirty inches, spreading habit, shade: This beautiful cultivar is unfortunately not hardy in zone 4, but other plants in this genus are, so if you are a zone 4 gardener, you might want to try the more winter hardy species: *A. canadensis, A. magellanica, A. nemerosa,* and *A. sylvestris.*

Though 'Robustissima' flowers for eight weeks or more from late August through October, its rich green foliage is at least as great an attraction. Grow grape-leaf anemone in shade and its lobed leaves will appear fresh and vigorous from spring until frost. They are remarkably pretty, making for a handsome attention-getting plant even when no bloom is present. The mauve-pink flowers are possessed of a shell-like delicacy and their lack of perfect symmetry somehow makes them particularly appealing. When the petals fall, the small hard centers remain, continuing to make texture in the garden. 'Robustissima' sometimes receives unflattering comments due to its propensity for enlarging its territory. Certainly by the third or fourth year you will need to root out portions that have crept in where they aren't wanted. The plus side is that 'Robustissima' makes a nice healthy clump and can be counted on to fill its allotted space completely, leaving no bare earth at its feet and contributing to a feeling of fullness in the border.

Be sure to give 'Robustissima' a shaded location. If planted where it receives direct sun for even part of the day it will suffer from midsummer on. Leaf edges brown and curl, thus destroying the beautiful foliage that should be one of the plant's chief assets.

A pair of *A.* x *hybrida* hardy to zone 4 are 'Honorine Jobert' and 'Whirlwind.' 'Honorine Jobert' has never been strong in my garden, though I have seen it doing well in a friend's zone 5 garden. For me, the elegant white flowers come on so late that they are routinely nipped by frost before full bloom is achieved. 'Whirlwind,' after three years in my garden, still hasn't formed a healthy clump or bloomed before frost. Both of these may fare better in zone 4, where extremes of heat are somewhat less severe.

Aster novae-angliae 'Andenken an Alma Pötschke,' syn. 'Alma Pötschke' (New England aster), perennial, height thirty-six inches, spread sixty inches or more, sun: For about seven weeks in late summer into fall, from about the beginning of September until frost, 'Alma Pötschke' is the show-stopping queen of the garden. When gardeners get together and talk shop, they refer to this big mama as Alma, as if she were a personal friend, possibly one with an operatic career. Certainly she is a force to be reckoned with. Around three feet tall at maturity in late summer, her matronly girth expands with age. A three-year-old plant is likely to span five feet in autumn. The width is exaggerated by her propensity to flop. A severe girdling of stakes and string might control her sloppy posture, but I have as yet been unable to fully accomplish it. This is a stunningly vigorous perennial.

To control Alma's size, you can dig and divide it every other spring. Although this means Alma is a bit on the high maintenance side, the good news is that the rate at which she grows means getting a free start from a garden friend should be easy. Pinching the plant tips two or three times in the spring and early summer is another way to control the size of a tall aster. Just nip off the last grouping of leaves on each stem when the plant is about six inches high. After every five or six inches of new growth, do it again, but stop pinching by mid-July to allow flower buds to develop. More drastic measures can be applied, if necessary. When massive spring rainfall made my 'Alma Pötschke' knee-high and floppy in June, I took shears to it and whacked it back to about four inches from the ground. By late summer the plant was a bushy but small specimen that bloomed very well.

However much digging, dividing, pinching, and whacking she requires, Alma justifies the effort. The hot pink blooms with which this beauty covers herself are eye-catching, to put it mildly. By mid-October, she is a mass of fiery pink that goes beautifully with the purples and lavenders of other fall asters, the pinks and lavenders of butterfly bushes, the pure white of *Boltonia as-*

teroides 'Snowbank,' the silver of *Artemisia stelleriana* (beach wormwood), and the white-hinting-at-blue of calamint.

Chrysanthemum, perennial, size varies, sun: The genus *Chrysanthemum* includes about twenty different species, but the common name is generally applied to the ubiquitous fall-blooming perennials available at garden centers. These plants can seem a nuisance in the garden all spring and through much of the summer when they are taking up quite a bit of space and not blooming at all. But just wait: In the fall they come into their glory just as many of your favorite perennials are bedding down for winter. Most chrysanthemums get going around the first of September and keep it up until the frost arrives, usually sometime in October.

Potted, blooming chrysanthemums are offered for sale in the fall. It's fun to buy them at this time because you can tell exactly what bloom color you're going to get. Just pop them out of their pots and into the ground for an instant splash of red, yellow, gold, orange, pink, purple, or white. Beware the darker red and purple flowers—they are likely to fade in our hot sun, often to an unpleasant brown. The potted plants won't put on any growth in fall, and you can't absolutely rely on their surviving the winter. Buy as early as possible to give the plants time to develop the root growth they will need to survive. Plant them in soil with good drainage and don't forget to water them often since their pot-size roots won't survive a dry stretch.

Chrysanthemums are said to require division every one to three springs to maintain their vigor. This involves digging the plant just after the leaves emerge, dividing it into pieces about three to six inches across, and replanting as many as you want to keep. Throw out the older inner part of the plant and keep only the newer outside sections. I used to do this with a lavender chrysanthemum that became leggy and flopped if not divided regularly, but I have a brilliant yellow plant that I never divide. It all depends. If your plants become lanky or bloom seems reduced from previous years, divide them. Anytime you want more plants, divide in spring. These plants grow so rapidly and are so easy to increase by division that buying more than one of a color is an extravagance. Buy just one and then increase your stock.

6

Providing Routine Care

Gardens are easiest in spring and early summer—young, tender, sweet, moist, and effortless. Weeds are mere seedlings, rain is adequate, diseases haven't yet gotten a foothold. This, too, is when many of the most beautiful flowers bloom—delicate, profuse and fragrant: *Convallaria* (lily-of-the-valley), *Narcissus* (daffodil), *Tulipa* (tulip), *Paeonia* (peony), irises, *Heuchera* (coral flower or coral bells), *Campanula* (bellflower), *Digitalis* (foxglove), *Viola* x *wittrockiana* (pansy), *Syringa* (lilac), roses. The garden is a delicate fairyland. It seems a paradise and you are in love with it. This is passionate young love when happily-ever-after seems not only attainable, but a lead pipe cinch.

Phase two—reality—hits around the end of June. "I've sort of lost interest in my garden," I heard someone say in July. Well, no wonder. It isn't all roses anymore. The weeds are up, the leaf miner has ravaged the *Aquilegia* (columbine), and mildew has overtaken the *Phlox divaricata* (woodland phlox or wild sweet William). Summer heat has struck the Midwest with its full blast, requiring endless watering. A gap in bloom between the spring flowers and the

late season ones has made the garden seem a wasteland. This is midlife crisis with a vengeance. The strong light of a summer day reveals the garden's every flaw. Autumn will roll around with cooler temperatures, renewed rain, truer colors shown under the sun's angled rays, and mature love will reap its reward. Staying power is the key in the midseason garden. Staying power means keeping on top of routine tasks like watering, weeding, and deadheading to see the garden through the heat of summer.

Weeding

Visitors to my garden often comment on how weed-free it is. In comparison to many flower gardens at midsummer or later it certainly is very clean, but I don't think I spend more time weeding than gardeners who feel they are up to their knees in weeds all the time. I simply do my weeding on a different schedule. If weeds are spotted and removed as seedlings, when they haven't yet put down deep roots, most of them are very easy to pull. The added benefit of moist ground makes springtime especially good for weeding. If weeds are pulled later in the year when they have established root systems, roots often snap off, leaving remnants behind to regenerate the plant. Another advantage of early attention to weeding is that weeds can be removed well before they go to seed, when they reproduce themselves by the hundreds and thousands.

Pulling weeds early doesn't mean you have to make time to go out and weed daily. Just keep an eagle eye out for weeds every time you step into your garden. As you water or cut flowers or put in annuals, watch for weeds and pull them the minute you see them. If you are diligent in scouring the garden for weeds in April, May, and June, you will be amazed at how few there are to deal with in the heat of summer. If you have been very lazy in the spring and find yourself surrounded by weeds in summer, get right on the job of removing them before they go to seed. The day after a rain the softer ground provides ideal weeding conditions. If you're facing a dry spell, plan to weed the day after a good watering.

Even desirable plants can be weeds if they are allowed to go to seed with abandon. If you are pressed for time, steer clear of annuals that go to seed very freely: *Cleome* (spider flower), *Consolida* (larkspur), *Borago officinalis* (borage), *Viola tricolor* (Johnny-jump-up), *Nicotiana alata,* syn. *N. affinis* (flowering tobacco), and others require a controlling hand to keep them from taking over.

To eliminate weeds, you need to be able to recognize them. This is essentially a process of elimination. Whatever is not a known desirable plant must be a weed. To recognize a weed, you first must know your own plants well. Each seedling, whether weed or garden plant, has a distinctive look. Learn that look for each desirable plant in your garden. Start by observing the appearance of the seedlings that emerge when you plant seeds. Notice, too, the sprinkling of seedlings that may appear around a mother plant after midsummer. By studying these you can learn to recognize flowers in their juvenile state. Once the true leaves begin to form, you should be able to see the resemblance to the foliage of mature plants. Don't forget that the nondescript cotyledons appear first. To avoid mistakes, wait until you're sure the first true leaves have appeared, otherwise you may pull a desirable seedling.

What about weeds that just can't be pulled? Some weeds or runaway ground covers, such as dandelions and *Aegopodium* (bishop's weed or goutweed), can be very persistent. No matter how carefully you pull them you always leave behind root fragments to restart the wretches. If these plants or other weeds become a problem in the cracks of pavement or in a gravel or wood chip path, there is an easy and nontoxic way to deal with them. Douse them with boiling water. The more persistent may need a second dousing a week or ten days later, but most will succumb the first time. If persistent weeds are growing among desirable plants, obviously you can't go sloshing about with boiling water. In some cases repeatedly pulling the same weed will progressively weaken and eventually eliminate it. In some situations, such as at the base of a shrub, you may be able to smother the weeds with thick layers of newspaper. A mulch of dirt or grass clippings thrown over the top will prevent the papers from blowing away. This will gradually smother the weeds and the paper will eventually rot into the ground.

A last resort in weed control is to use Roundup carefully. This herbicide will kill everything it touches. The plant absorbs the Roundup into its system through its leaves and slowly, over a period of one to three weeks, dies. Even this harsh treatment may sometimes have to be repeated to fully kill the most determined weeds. Roundup is most effective used in warm weather when plants are growing rapidly. Obviously, since this spray will kill any plant material it touches, you endanger your desirable plants by using it. For this reason you need to exercise great care when spraying it. If you apply it in even the slightest breeze you may kill nearby plants. Wind drift, sloppy spraying, or even wetting a weed that is touching another plant can do considerable damage. This product is also expensive, so use it sparingly and consider other weed removal methods first.

Watering

Appropriate watering is crucial to the survival of a landscape in our hot climate. This is perhaps the most difficult part of the gardener's art to teach through words alone. To a great extent, you just have to get out there and learn it by trial and error.

Flowering plants need at least an inch of water a week. When temperatures are well above 90 degrees, they'll need more. Buy a rain gauge and check it routinely so that you know how much rain your garden is getting. Even though the local weather report tells you how much rain has fallen in your general area, rain can be very spotty, so you should check the rain in your own yard yourself.

When you receive less than an inch a week, you must water. Because they are protected from rain, plants under the eaves of your house or tucked in around tree roots will require watering even during rainy periods. Assessing your garden's need for water is complicated by windy conditions, which dry plants and cause them to need additional moisture.

Soaking a bed thoroughly and letting it dry out is preferable to watering lightly and frequently. This is common advice handed out in garden books. Take it with a grain of salt, because our region's peak summer heat and wind can make actually soaking a bed a near impossibility. Reality comes into play when several consecutive windy days over 95 degrees occur and you just have to get out there and apply all the water you can whenever you can do it.

Plants in sun will normally wilt somewhat during the heat of the afternoon and freshen up in the relative cool of the evening. They look their best and make the nicest cut flowers first thing in the morning when they have had all night to restore moisture to all parts of the plant. Drooping leaves at noon on a hot day do not necessarily mean that water is needed because the plant is simply not pumping water as rapidly as it is losing it. As the sun goes down, the plant will catch up. Overcast skies will slow drying, but under sunny skies more moisture is required. There's a difference between wilting and shriveling, however. Wrinkled leaves, crisp leaf edges, a whole plant lying loose on the ground are all signs of imminent death. The plant requires immediate water and possibly some temporary shade—an upended box or bushel basket or even a leafy twig stuck in the ground next to the plant.

The toughest plants that require little water, such as *Hemerocallis* (daylily), tall bearded irises, *Baptisia australis* (blue wild indigo, false indigo, or plains false indigo), and *Epimedium* (barrenwort) show little if any drooping during periods of drought. Many gray plants (those with a downy surface) are native on dry land and do best if scarcely watered. Even though they tend to wilt in heat, they still probably don't need water. Examples are *Achillea* 'Moonshine' (yarrow), *Lychnis coronaria* (rose campion), *Artemisia stelleriana* (beach wormwood), and *Stachys byzantina*, syn. *S. lanata* (lamb's-ears).

The ideal time to water is morning. Pump the plants full of water so they can get through the heat of the day. Watering in the evening is second best, but may promote fungus. If you have a busy schedule, evening may be your only choice and is better than not watering at all. Midafternoon is not a good time to water because the Midwestern wind will evaporate an enormous amount of what you apply. Even the gentle spray of sprinkler or hose nozzle may cause plants limp from the heat to collapse into the mud.

Shade plants, like *Astilbe* (false spirea) and *Hosta* (hosta or plantain lily), tend to be moisture lovers, but they require less frequent watering than other plants because the lack of sun helps keep them from drying out. The exception to this rule is the dreaded dry shade. Shaded slopes and areas under mature trees, especially evergreens, are likely to be very dry. You can improve the situation by thorough soil preparation and removal of a few tree roots. Adding the humus that shade plants love will create a rich and moisture-retentive soil.

Water each plant at its base as much as possible to help control fungus, to avoid squashing limp plants, and to get more water to the roots. Plants that are especially prone to fungus should never be watered on their leaves: roses, delphiniums, zinnias, *Monarda* (bee balm or bergamot), *Phlox paniculata* (garden phlox), and lilacs. A drip irrigation system is one way to provide water without dampening leaves. Arrange soaker hoses around plants in early spring when they are small. When the garden needs moisture, allow water to drip from the soaker hoses for an extended period of time. This soaks the ground deeply without allowing water to dampen foliage or evaporate.

Plants do soak up water through their leaves and stems, so those not prone to fungus can be refreshed quickly with a light sprinkling if they are excessively stressed by heat and hot wind. Hose attachments that fan water are beneficial because they soften the spray so that you aren't knocking plants down with a stiff blast of water and creating a muddy splatter. The watering attachment that looks like a shower head on a wand is very useful for extending your reach. A shut-off valve for the hose end allows you to turn the water off for limited periods of time without returning to the tap. Avoid using this hose end shutoff for long periods, though, as the water pressure created can cause a hose to spring a leak. A timer can be attached at the tap to set water to run for a specific time and then shut off. This is handy if you want to water in the morning but must leave for work before the watering can be completed.

Soil cracks will open in areas of packed soil during periods of drought. This allows water to penetrate a hard crust. You can't fill the cracks with water and it is useless and a waste of water to try. Water will soak into loose soil best. Create a loose soil to begin with, enriching it with lots of organic material. Mulch it lightly. When the surface of your beds hardens, cultivate lightly with a hoe before watering. This will keep the water from simply rolling off.

Although it is difficult to water too much in our usually hot and dry summers, it can be done by the determined greenhorn. To avoid this, pay attention to the specific wants of your plants. Irises want it hot and dry, as do most herbs. Prepare your soil in the first place so that it is loose and free draining. Don't water in any week when an inch or more of rain has fallen unless temperatures are above 90 degrees. Don't water every time a plant droops. Remember that it takes only an inch of water to penetrate five inches of soil.

The smaller the plant, the more often it will need water. Established trees seldom require irrigation, although a sustained summer drought will require a fall soaking to take trees into winter. Shrubs need weekly watering in their first one or two growing seasons. After that only extended dry spells will necessitate watering.

After a long rainy period, flowering plants wilt and droop almost at once when weather turns dry. It's a temptation to water them even though the ground is saturated. This may be necessary if wilting is severe, but a light sprinkling will usually suffice. Normally, though, plants snap back when the cool of evening arrives. My very unscientific idea is that more than adequate rain makes plants lazy. They haven't put their roots down deep enough to find moisture when incessant rain finally stops. After a few days without rain, plants shift gears, plunge their roots down deeper, and adjust.

The same sort of thing happens if you water excessively, particularly in the spring when you first put plants in the ground. The first week after planting you should probably water annuals and small perennials daily. After a week or two this frequent watering isn't needed and in fact seems to discourage the deep root production plants need to see them through the heat of summer.

Container plants require daily watering in hot weather. Extreme heat— above 95 degrees—may necessitate watering twice a day. Double watering may be needed even at lower temperatures on windy days. This frequent watering leaches nutrients out of the soil, however, so give container plants a liquid fertilizer according to package instructions. Pot plants need bottom drainage to carry off excess water. If for some reason you want the container to sit in a saucer, you'll need to empty the saucer immediately after each watering or rain because a plant left sitting in water will soon expire.

Mulching

You can seriously improve your garden's ability to retain moisture by applying a mulch in the spring after planting. This should be done about midspring after all bulbs and perennials have shown themselves above the soil's surface and annuals have been planted. There are a number of materials you can use for mulch, many of them on sale at garden shops. Bark, cocoa hulls, and straw are examples. You're better off, in my opinion, to use a couple of mulches that are available free on your own property.

Compost can be used as mulch if it is well rotted and fine textured, applied thinly (about one inch), and hoed in lightly. If not thoroughly rotted, though, compost can actually impede water penetration. An alternative is to mulch with grass clippings. Getting rid of them is probably a headache anyway. Why not put them to work? Apply an inch or two of grass clippings around all your plants, being careful not to put them against plant stems, as the heat of decomposing grass can burn the stalks.

A fresh mulch of green grass clippings looks a little strange at first, but within a few days it turns brown and fades into the background. Rain soaks through it easily. It gradually rots down and adds humus to the soil, and as it gets too thin you can just replace it with new clippings.

When a plant is a bit faint of heart, a winter mulch can help pull it through the cold part of the year. If your yard has mature deciduous trees, you'll find that nature provides the mulch for you. The leaves that drop in autumn will blow freely across your smooth lawn to catch on the stalks of plants in your flower beds. Come spring, about eight weeks before the last frost, you can rake the leaves off. Don't strip the beds bare in one afternoon, but peel back a layer at a time in two or three raking sessions over a week or more. You'll avoid shocking the tender shoots making their way out of the ground, and it's easier on your back, too. But be careful: if you wait too long to accomplish this spring cleanup, the weight of the leaves may flatten emerging bulb foliage.

Pinching and Deadheading

Pinching in early spring encourages a plant to branch, creating a fuller form and additional bloom. In some cases it reduces flopping of typically large and untidy plants. Asters and chrysanthemums become bushier and more upright with this treatment, as do zinnias. You can pinch any plant that has a branching habit. To pinch, simply wait until the plant has at least three sets of true leaves. Then pinch or snip off the terminal leaves and the stem end to just above the next set of leaves down. The plant will branch at this point. You can pinch again after the branches have two or three sets of leaves.

For full and tidy growth, some plants respond well to shearing. Use shears or a big pair of scissors to take off no more than about one-third the height of the plant. Plants that form basal clumps (all of their leaves springing individually from one center with no branching) are not suitable for either pinching or shearing. Examples of this type of plant are hostas and *Pulmonaria* (lungwort). *Iberis sempervirens* (candytuft) tends to suffer some winterkill and can be shorn back to green wood. It will then put on a spring growth that soon makes a nice bushy plant. Following bloom, shear it again to encourage fresh foliage. Some plants, like *Nepeta* (catmint), are such prolific bloomers that removing spent flowers individually isn't practical. For these, shearing when bloom wanes is appropriate and may spur a second wave of flowering. *Coreopsis verticillata* 'Moonbeam' (threadleaf tickseed) is often suggested for shearing, but you may find that it does just as well without. In my garden it takes a vacation in late summer, but then blooms again without a haircut.

You must deadhead (remove spent flowers to prevent seed production) routinely. Just a few minutes of deadheading tidies up individual plants and creates a striking improvement in the attractiveness of your flower beds. Deadheading also prevents seed formation, which forces the plant to bloom again in an attempt to produce more seeds. In some plants increased blooming is especially dramatic. Pansies and rose campion are nonstop bloomers if you make the effort to cut off old bloom regularly. In other plants, a first wave of bloom will be followed by a second and smaller, but still handsome bloom, if you remember to cut back the first bloom. Yarrow, foxgloves, and *Gypsophila paniculata* (baby's breath) will all produce that second ripple if deadheaded promptly.

Walk around your garden regularly to remove old bloom, making sure to take the swelling base of the blossom, where seed will form. Collect spent blooms in a grocery bag or basket for the compost bin. If you fall behind on deadheading and seed heads have formed, don't put them on the compost or you may have to contend with thousands of seedlings in the garden next spring. (If compost becomes hot enough in the rotting process, seed will be killed, but don't rely on this happening.) Some plants are easily deadheaded by simply pinching or snapping off the bloom head, but with others you'll need scissors or pruning shears.

Deadheading is best accomplished daily on very prolific bloomers. If you have a large garden, deadheading is a big chore, but doing it daily makes it easier to keep up with it. It can become especially tedious when dealing with really prolific bloomers like petunias, flowering tobacco, or rose campion, but the effort is well worth it, in terms of both additional bloom and the greatly improved appearance of your garden and each plant in it. Deadhead tulips and daffodils promptly so that they put their energy into the bulb that will produce next year's bloom. Leaving the seed heads to develop can rob the bulb of a third of its vigor.

With a few plants, seed formation is desirable to foster reproduction and naturalization. (Naturalization is nothing but the natural formation of a colony through the scattering of a plant's own seed.) *Galanthus nivalis* (common snowdrop), for instance, will gradually spread if left to form seed, as will *Scilla siberica* (Siberian squill), *Chionodoxa luciliae*, syn. *C. gigantea* (glory of the snow), and some *Lilium* (lily). I am very fond of Johnny-jump-ups and allow them to go to seed with abandon. They are such champion bloomers that they don't seem to suffer from the lack of deadheading, and each spring I have a fresh new crop. *Mertensia pulmonarioides,* syn. *M. virginica* (Virginia bluebells) is a lovely thing in the spring garden before it politely steps out of the way by going dormant. I allow it to go to seed because I want to encourage its spread. Likewise,

I never deadhead *Geum triflorum* (prairie smoke), as I want to see the charming little whorls of fuzz its seed heads make. With some short-lived perennials, I may deadhead most of the bloom to keep the plant neat and floriferous, but I allow some seed to form and self-sow to replace the plants that will inevitably die out. Columbines and *Corydalis lutea*, syn. *Pseudofumaria lutea* fall into this category. Some roses form absolutely gorgeous seed heads called hips in late summer. If you want these to develop, stop deadheading midsummer. Try it once to see which roses in your garden make attractive hips. You may find that a lovely pink rose makes a brash orange hip that in no way fits your color scheme. On the other hand, your favorite rose may produce burnished red hips the size of crabapples. You just don't know till you try.

Edging

Maintaining a neat appearance goes a long way toward making a beautiful impression with your flower bed. Edging material will prevent massive invasion by grass, which can be the worst possible weed in a perennial border. No matter what edging material you choose to place as a barrier between flower garden and lawn, some grass will eventually invade. If you edge with stone or brick merely laid in place, once a year you need to lift the edging bit by bit and beat back the intruding lawn. The best time to do this (or to install edging in the first place) is very early in the season when there is little else you can do. I'm talking about that frustrating period about six to ten weeks before the frost-free date when spring signs like crocuses in flower, greening grass, and birds pairing off make a gardener yearn to get going. It's too early to plant perennials or prune, but you can get your annual edging done. It's a good time for it, because later in the season plants at the front of the bed will billow over the edging, making your job more difficult.

Start at one end of the bed and lift a couple of feet of edging. Then take a sharp shovel and jam it into the ground at the outer rim. This will cut off the encroaching grass. Lift to loosen the roots and spreading shoots. Remove them, crumbling excess dirt back into the ground. Then even up the surface and replace the edging material. Repeat along the entire length of edging.

You may have something more permanent in the way of edging, such as stone or brick set in concrete. This forms a more lasting barrier, but as cracks develop, the grass will still manage to creep in. In early spring, push a shovel into the earth at the outer rim of the edging to cut off any roots and shoots trying to get in. Later in the season, when the weather has warmed up, you can use Roundup to kill any bits that have made their way through to the garden side.

Staking

If you don't want your garden to look like a carpet under your feet, you have to throw a few tall plants into the design mix. This creates a problem since very few really stately perennials are going to stand up on their own to the wind that is commonplace in our area, especially when it's combined with heat. You will need to stake. Those pictures you see in gardening books of masses of unstaked foxgloves towering over the mixed border were probably taken in England. They were most certainly not taken in the hot and windy farm belt.

There are a number of ways to accomplish proper staking. The easiest approach is to buy appropriate plant stakes. For plants with a few big bloom stalks, like tall bearded irises, a simple metal rod with an unclosed loop on one end is just the ticket. For tall, bushy plants, grow-through supports that look like a grid mounted on three or four metal rods are handy. You put the support in place over the young plant and simply allow the plant to grow up and through the grid. As foliage develops the grid becomes hidden. This is a very useful kind of support, but also a very expensive one. Less costly is a simple arrangement of two fixed hoops on metal rods. Designed for peonies, these might also be used for asters and other small to midsize bushy plants.

Bamboo stakes can be purchased relatively cheaply in various lengths and used in a number of ways. A tall bamboo stake can be plunged into the ground near each bloom stalk of a regal plant like a delphinium or tall lily. You can then use string to attach the stake to the stalk at three or four points. Arrange the string in a figure 8, with one loop of the 8 around the plant. To close the other loop of the 8 you'll secure the loose ends of the string around the stake with a square knot. Keeping the string loose prevents strangling the plant stalk. This is tricky work. You can make it much easier by using a tip my stepfather, a retired doctor, taught me. As you wrap one end of the string around the other to form the first half of your knot, wrap it around one extra time. Then pull it into place. That extra wrap prevents the first half of the knot from slipping while you form the second half. Apparently surgeons use this method when tying sutures.

I recommend a square knot because it won't slide and come loose in a stiff wind. If you are pathologically incapable of tying a square knot, I offer this advice: right over and under left, then left over and under right. Lead with your right hand as you tie the first half of the knot, going over first, then under. Then lead with your left hand as you tie the second half, again going over, then under. You'll come out with a perfect square knot every time. Confused? Pretend you're tying your shoelaces—the motions are the same.

Bamboo stakes can also be used to form a stout girdling cage for midsize bushy plants. When the foliage is six or eight inches high in the spring, surround the plant closely with half a dozen two-foot bamboo stakes (a sharp pair of pruning shears will make the cutting easy). Jam them well into the ground, leaving about eighteen inches above ground (or enough to equal about half of the plant's mature height). Wrap string around the stakes starting about four inches above the ground and repeating every four or five inches.

Wind the string around two or three times to make it good and stout. As the stems grow taller, make sure they stay inside the cage. The plant will soon fill in and hide the cage. This system works very well for baby's breath and asters and might also be used for peonies if you don't want to invest in a commercially sold peony ring.

Pea staking can support small to medium-size plants prone to flopping. Pea stakes are twiggy branches that you gather in spring from prunings or from dead wood that has fallen from trees or shrubs. They need to be stiff but not so brittle that moderate pressure makes them shatter. Just jam the stem ends into the ground all around the base of a plant and let it grow up through the pea stakes. Climbing plants that will be trained onto a trellis sometimes have a tough time getting started. Pea staking can provide them with an easy boost up onto the trellis.

The key to proper staking is to start early before the plant actually begins to topple. Provide staking sturdy enough to handle the plant at mature size when it is being whipped by wind. Use care not to push stakes and rods into underground roots and bulbs, especially when you're staking lilies.

Pruning

Pruning woody plants is another routine task that helps to keep your garden looking its best, but this one needs to be done only annually at most. You should prune to encourage the plant to have a shape you find attractive or to keep bloom from occurring above your head where you can't enjoy it. Pruning is complicated because different plants have different growth patterns, but a good book on the subject can offer guidance when you decide it's time to prune. Basically, you want to cut just above a leaf bud or the point where a twig meets a main stem of the branch, because this is where a shoot of new growth will develop.

Pruning to make a bush the shape you want is one thing. Pruning to keep a bush smaller than its natural size is quite another. Constant pruning to reduce the size may ultimately reduce the vigor of the shrub and will give it a butchered look. It's better to allow shrubs the vertical and horizontal space they'll need for their full mature growth.

Standard size lilacs, however, respond well to frequent pruning. Without pruning, they will soon be blooming far above your head. To keep them at eye (and nose) level, you'll need to cut them back every three to five years soon after they bloom. If you wait too long or cut them back in spring before bloom, you'll eliminate the flowering for one season. Lilacs put on a good foot or more of growth the first season after pruning, so cut them well back. I like to trim mine down to about four feet high. Simply use pruning shears to cut all branches off at one level. Then use a saw to cut off any stout, tough old stems at the ground. The bush will soon put on fresh growth and look lush again. An old lilac that is very overgrown can be cut back completely to just above the ground. It will regenerate quickly to produce more bloom on a better-looking bush. Lilacs like sun, though, so if an old overgrown lilac is in a shady position due to maturing of nearby trees, it may not do well after a severe pruning.

Forsythia, too, should be pruned back immediately following bloom. Do this when the shrub is getting too large or when bloom diminishes. The wrong way to prune a forsythia is to hack it all back to one uniform height. This is no way to treat an elegant lady. Take the time to prune branches individually to varying lengths to maintain a graceful appearance. The shrub will spring back quickly, so prune a good foot or two below where you want it to be after it begins to grow again.

Roses should be pruned in spring about four to six weeks before the frost-free date. If you do the job earlier, late winter cold is almost sure to kill the plant back further and you'll find yourself repeating the task. Moderate temperatures and blooming crocuses make it very difficult to exercise self-control in this matter. I can assure you from personal experience of succumbing to the temptation to prune on the first warm February or March day that you will do better to wait. When the time is right, prune off all dead wood. If you're not sure what is dead, snip off a little at a time until you can see the green inside the cane, which indicates you have reached live wood. Once the dead wood is off, shape the bush as you want it. In general, cut just above a shoot that is headed in the direction you want the branch to go. Once the plant is in bloom, prune as you deadhead or cut flowers for bouquets by cutting back to just above any leaf that has five leaflets. This is a simplified treatment of a subject that takes up whole chapters in rose books.

When pruning *Hydrangea* and clematis, look to see whether they flower on last year's growth that survived winter or on growth made during the current year. Shrubs that flower on the previous season's growth must be pruned *after* they flower (unless you're willing to sacrifice a year's bloom). If the plant flowers on the current year's growth, you can prune it in spring, along with the roses, about four to six weeks before the frost-free date.

Some shrubs will live through winter to grow larger and larger in milder climates, but in our area they will die back. *Buddleia davidii* (butterfly bush) and *Callicarpa* (beautyberry) are two examples for zone 5. Both grow rapidly enough to make a small shrub each year, so cut them back near ground level in spring.

Many shrubs require only moderate occasional pruning to keep them in the shape you desire. *Viburnum,* for instance, is a handsome family of shrubs whose members grow naturally into nicely shaped bushes, suffering from little or no winter dieback. Given adequate space, these will require very little pruning.

Pest and Disease Control

All of us have in our heads visions of garden perfection toward which we strive. We want our own gardens to match the vision. It's easy to get the idea that any problem in the garden can be dealt with given enough time, energy, spray, dust, fertilizer, fungicide, and money. What's really needed is a liberal dose of realism. Even the most carefully tended garden will have its share of fungus, insect pests, sudden deaths of seemingly healthy plants, disappointing bloom, drought-damaged foliage, rabbits, squirrels, hail and wind damage. A great deal is beyond your control, and many of the controls available to you are dangerous to the natural world you love so much. It's good to remember that perfection is what you aim for, not what you expect to achieve.

Do your best to site plants well and provide them the care that will promote their good health. When garden plans don't pan out, remind yourself that this is nature you're dealing with. It's big, it's unpredictable, it's about death as well as life, and it's beyond your control. In spite of your best efforts, zinnias will mildew late in the season, columbines will be stricken with leaf miners, roses will suffer disease, hostas will be savaged by slugs. Your garden picture—after the first blush of spring—will always include at least one unsightly problem or another. Provide the best care you can, but recognize that sometimes when a problem arises, your best course is to ignore it.

When it comes to pest control, the question is, To spray or not to spray? I am not a proponent of organic gardening, but I do believe that a healthy, luxuriant garden can be achieved with mostly natural methods and scant use of commercial fertilizers, sprays, or fungicides. This view of things began to be shaped one year when I decided I would get ahead of the game, pest-wise. I would spray for insects on a regular basis and would not have to cope with leaf miners or tarnished plant bugs. I was consistent about preventive sprayings but the garden was more plagued by insects than it had ever been. I think I quite simply upset the balance of nature in my little garden ecosystem. Still, if you're not going to spray, how will you handle pest control? Here are a few suggestions.

Slugs and Snails

Slugs and snails are damaging pests that are difficult to dispatch. They are mollusks, not insects, belonging to the same family as the clams you like to stir into chowder. In fact, I once saw a magazine article on trapping snails that included a recipe for cooking them with garlic and butter. Disgusting as it sounds, the best way to get rid of snails is to handpick them and crush them. You can use your thumbnail on small ones and step on the larger specimens. You can't be squeamish and be a gardener.

Larger and far more common are slugs. These slimy, oozing pests amount to snails without the cute little shells. Tiny young slugs are hardly visible. Older slugs, thoroughly fattened on your precious hostas and stretched out as they ooze their way toward another succulent morsel, are as long as four inches.

Snails and slugs feed in the cool of the night, so they are most commonly seen in the garden in the early morning or at twilight. They eat by scraping against plant leaves with their rasplike mouths. During the day, when they are not busy defiling your garden, they hide out in cool, moist, dark cracks and crevices. I often find them huddled up against the cool stone edging of my borders. They prefer shade, cool weather, and moist conditions.

The relatively small number of snails in Midwestern gardens makes them a minor concern, but slugs can become a serious threat. They are dreadful pests on hostas and will also attack a wide range of other plants, including daylilies and pansies.

A frequently recommended slug control method is what I call the slug beer bust. You sink shallow bowls or tuna cans into the garden until their lips are roughly level with the soil surface. The bowls are then filled with beer. The slugs find the scent so bewitching that they slide into the beer for a drink and drown. I do not recommend this means of control. In the first place, it is quite revolting when the beer and slug corpses ferment into a foamy, syrupy, foul-smelling hell-broth that you must dispose of somehow. When I was hosting these beer parties, I buried the old beer and dead slug mix before refilling the containers. The whole process was nasty, nasty, nasty. Still, I kept doing it because there seemed to be an upswing in the slug population and the little sots were becoming a serious problem.

The scent of beer will entice slugs from a very wide area, however, and actually attracts far more slugs to your garden than it kills. This would explain why, in spite of my best efforts with the beer traps, my slug population was thriving. No doubt my neighbors were congratulating themselves on the sudden reduction in the number of slugs in their yards. Every slug in the vicinity had pulled up stakes and headed for my beer garden.

Another commonly suggested method for controlling slugs is a slug bait called Slug-Geta manufactured by Ortho. Available at garden centers, it is moderately successful in limiting the number of slugs in your garden but does not get rid of them completely. It has to be more or less fresh, so every time you get a good rain you have to put out more of it. The chief drawback, though, is that the bait looks enough like dog food to be dangerously attractive to wandering canines. Birds may also be at risk, but cats seem uninterested in the pellets. Slug-Geta is poisonous to humans, too, so using it in a garden visited by small children would be unwise. I use slug bait only very occasionally when slugs get out of hand and begin to cause widespread damage.

My preferred method of controlling slugs is simply to kill them by hand. My husband calls this the two-brick method. When I spot a slug, I pick it up with a stick or a stiff leaf and transfer it to a hard surface, where I either step on it or squash it with a brick. This is a very effective treatment. If I happen to be trimming or deadheading when I spot a slug, I use my pruning shears to cut the slug in half or at least nick its surface. Slugs do not recover from this strategy. Another method of dispatching slugs is to coat the inside of a plastic milk carton with oil. Handpick the slugs from your garden and drop them into the milk bottle. The slippery sides keep them from escaping. When you finish, screw on the cap and throw the bottle in the trash.

Anytime I have reason to turn back a stone in the edging of my garden, I take a look to see if slugs are sheltering there and quickly dispatch any I find. In spring I watch for eggs around hostas and other plants that were attacked by slugs the previous year. The eggs are small, round, and transparent like tiny bubbles and can be easily destroyed by smashing them. These hand methods with occasional use of slug bait (perhaps once a year) seem to keep the slug population within reason.

Aphids

Aphids are common garden pests that you are likely to come up against every year. They cluster on stems and suck the juices from young tender tips. There are many kinds in several colors: green, red, pink, black, gray, and so on. These soft-bodied and usually wingless creatures secrete a sticky substance called honeydew, which attracts ants. You may notice a shiny spattering of this dried honeydew on leaves or find ants around stem ends. You may see wilting on young growth at tips. These are signs that you should examine the plant for aphids.

Aphids are common pests on roses, but they attack a wide range of other plants, too. In my garden they routinely prey on a dwarf crabapple and *Echinops ritro* (small globe thistle). They also occasionally go after the ivy among my container plants.

The simplest way to rid plants of aphids is to first shoot off what you can with a strong squirt of water from the hose (but not on roses, which do not appreciate wet leaves in a humid climate). Then simply squash any remaining aphids by pinching them against the plant stem or between thumb and forefinger. Rinse the plant (and your hands!) with the hose and keep a close eye on it over the next several days, watching for any return. If aphids continue to be a problem, you can use Raid House and Garden spray for further control. Because aphids attack new growth, you need only the small amount of spray it takes to treat the tips. I prefer not to spray if I can help it because spraying risks killing aphid predators like ladybugs.

Other Insect Pests

Many other pests will occasionally visit your garden. They may be a serious threat in one year and hardly noticeable the next. Weather and climate conditions—an especially hard winter or an exceptionally rainy spring—may affect their ability to reproduce and result in a bumper crop one year and a complete absence the next. When you do discover insect pests on your plants, first determine that they are indeed pests and not beneficial or harmless insects. Then start with the easiest, cheapest, and most environmentally sound method of pest control. Simply remove them by hand and squash them. If this is not effective, you need to assess whether the pests are seriously damaging your plants or the appearance of your garden. Is the damage temporary or life threatening? Try to put up with a certain amount of damage, but if havoc is being wrought you may have to take steps.

Before you use any insecticide, determine exactly what kind of insect you are dealing with. If you are unable to identify it by consulting reference books, seek expert advice. The best way to do this is to capture an insect and take it, along with a cutting from the plant that shows the damage it is suffering, to your local nursery. This, of course, assumes that a trained staff is on hand. If this is not the case, consult your cooperative extension service or county extension office. Having identified the specific culprit, use a spray that will kill it. Not all sprays kill all insects, but labels clearly identify which insects a spray is designed to control. Be sure to read the entire label to see what harmless or useful insects will also be killed by the spray. If the insecticide you plan to use will kill off every bee in your yard, you may want to think twice.

Squirrels and Rabbits

Squirrels and rabbits can do enormous amounts of damage. Young trees and shrubs will die if enough of their bark is chewed off, so the immature trunks will need to be wrapped or protected in cages of chicken wire or hardware cloth. A gardening friend of mine tells me that squirrels and rabbits chew young bark to get moisture and will be less destructive if water is set out on the ground for them, but I've had mixed results after following her advice.

Rabbits will chew off the new leaves and buds of crocuses. They also like the tender young shoots of just about anything green, including new growth on shrubs. A simple prevention is to place pine boughs around plants they seem to be targeting. Rabbits apparently don't appreciate having their noses prickled while they snack. If you don't have pines in your yard, recycle a Christmas tree for the purpose. Slivers of soap stuck part way into the ground around a plant victim can help deter rabbits, too, as can a scattering of yew clippings.

Squirrels are especially partial to the buds of clematis. A choice *Clematis* 'Nelly Moser,' planted against a fence, provided a gourmet buffet of some sixty succulent buds one spring, leaving me with a paltry three or four blooms. A mix of hot pepper sauce and water sprayed onto the vine may make the buds distasteful to the squirrels. Both squirrels and rabbits will break off plant stems, sometimes apparently just from curiosity. There is little you can do to prevent this damage, but as plants mature they become sturdier and less vulnerable.

Fungus

Various symptoms caused by fungus may appear on your plants, chiefly leaf spot, powdery mildew, and rust. Leaf spots are relatively easy to identify because, as the name suggests, they make clearly defined spots. If the spotting is widespread it is called leaf blight. Leaf spot is especially common among roses and irises. You encourage fungus when you crowd plantings, water plants from above, plant sun lovers in shady places, or allow diseased foliage to remain in the garden through winter.

Rust is a fungal disease characterized by leaves spotty on their surface and covered on the underside with spore pustules. The spores are likely to be rust colored (hence the name), but may also be brown, black, white, yellow, or orange. Good garden cleanup in the fall to remove affected foliage will help retard the spread of rust. As with leaf spot, overhead watering should be avoided. Rust may exist without seriously damaging its host, so before spraying decide whether the disease is truly harming the plant. A wide variety of perennials may be attacked by this disease, including *Anemone,* columbines, *Campanula* (bellflower), clematis, delphiniums, and *Monarda* (bee balm or bergamot).

Powdery mildew, a common problem, attacks both *Phlox paniculata* (garden phlox) and *Phlox divaricata* (woodland phlox or wild sweet William), as well as zinnias, *Monarda,* asters, and many other flowering plants. Splotches of a grayish, finely textured substance indicate the presence of powdery mildew. The disease first appears in the summer months when soaring heat and humidity encourage its growth. As with other fungal disease, prevention methods include removal of diseased plant materials in fall, watering from below, and avoidance of overcrowded plantings. Ironically, fungus—which you might expect to find in damp places—actually thrives when plants are too dry, so for prevention, be sure to keep plants adequately moist.

Fungal diseases can be so persistent and damaging that they may require spraying. Attempt to identify the specific problem and seek expert advice if you can't. Choose an appropriate spray and read the label carefully before you buy it.

7

Troubleshooting

"I don't have a green thumb" is the biggest cop-out in horticulture. There is no such thing as a green thumb—some sort of God-given gardening gift. As with any talent, good gardening begins with a personal predilection and develops with study and practice. To be a good gardener, just read, ask questions, and get your hands dirty.

If you are unhappy with the garden you have made, the trouble probably started with one or more of these problems:

1. You haven't properly prepared your soil. You are turning the soil but not amending it or, worse yet, you are just digging a hole in your turf, shoving in a plant, and expecting it to flourish. Chapter 3 is your soil preparation Bible. Read it, do it, and marvel at the results.

2. You've chosen plants that are not winter hardy for your zone. This is a simple question of not doing your homework before buying plants, especially those acquired by mail order. Most of what you buy locally is suitable for your zone, although nurseries do sell a

few plants that are one zone off for enthusiasts willing to make the extra effort in winter protection and take the risk of loss.

3. You're trying to raise plants that are winter hardy where you live but can't stand the heat of a Midwestern summer. Consult chapter 5 for help.

4. You've failed to meet the light and soil requirements of the plants you are attempting to grow: you've planted shade lovers in sun, plants that require good drainage in unprepared clay soil, sun lovers against a north wall.

5. You are putting plants in the ground too early or too late.

6. You plant too closely, ignoring the plant's mature size. It's a great temptation in spring, when emerging plants are small, to tuck in just one more plant. The result is overcrowding, poor bloom, and disease.

7. You are watering too much or too little—much more likely too little in our hot climate. Lack of water will reduce bloom, dwarf plants, disfigure foliage, encourage fungus, and can, in times of drought, kill plants. Too much water, if you somehow manage to overwater, can drown plants and wash away nutrients.

8. You've ignored routine care, such as deadheading, pruning, and weeding. Neglect in these matters will produce an untidy and unappealing garden.

9. You've set impossibly high standards for your garden. The garden isn't a failure, but your perception of it is.

Like life, a garden is not perfection, but a striving toward it. Even the glorious gardens in books aren't the perfection they appear. One of the big lies of garden literature is that a perennial garden can be created without gap or flaw. The truth is that the right camera angle can hide the problems that occur in even the best plantings. The loveliest garden is transient, and the gardens pictured in books are not as lovely as they appear even at the instant the camera clicks. However, take heart. Your garden will make progress toward perfection as you read, try new plants, discard the inferior, redesign beds, divide and increase favorites, and so on. Every mistake you make teaches you something about the art of gardening.

Flat on My Face

For your inspiration and edification I offer the sad story of one of my own failures. Although this was one of my earliest efforts in the garden, the failure lingered accusingly at the top of my gently sloping backyard for several years until finally a disastrous storm damaged trees so seriously that I was forced to relandscape the whole area.

The problem began as an inherited failure—an ill-conceived flower border that was in place when I moved into my house twenty-one years ago. The bed was about five feet deep and thirty feet long, planted with three lilacs spaced nine feet apart. Between these shrubs were peonies and daylilies. Unfortunately, the entire combination lay squarely in the considerable shade of an oak tree that was more than twenty years old. All of these plants prefer to be sited in full sun and probably were until the oak began to come into its own. In the oak's shade the lilacs bloomed only fitfully and the peonies and daylilies not at all. Poor siting, then, was the first mistake.

To make matters worse, the previous gardener (I had nothing to do with this) had planted three different kinds of lilacs together—one of them fan-shaped, one upright and bushy, and one upright but bare at its feet and knees with most of the foliage beginning about four feet above ground level. As a result of the shade and their incompatible forms, these three never formed the hedge or screen that was probably intended, making instead sadly unattractive companions.

This is where I came on the scene. I noticed that the bed seemed never to have been dug over and the dirt was hard and unyielding.

Even in these early days of my gardening apprenticeship I recognized that the daylilies would never bloom on a densely shaded site. I decided to remove them, enjoy the peonies for their foliage, dig over the rest of the bed, and plant shade-loving *Hosta* (hosta or plantain lily). The result was a miserable flop. My ideas were all right, but they didn't go far enough.

First, I thought preparing a bed meant simply digging it over to loosen the soil. I didn't add compost. I didn't work in bonemeal or gypsum. In short, I did nothing to keep the soil from turning back into a hard moisture-repellent medium after a few hard rains. I then compounded my error by planting hostas—plants that demand a rich, loose, moist soil. Because the bed was on a slight incline, there was even less chance that rain would soak in to root depth. The hostas never reached anything like the full size and vigor that the same variety achieved elsewhere in properly prepared soil.

I also erred in thinking I could remove the daylilies by simply digging out each clump. Daylilies are survivors. It is no accident that they can be found thriving around uninhabited old farmhouses. I should have dug and removed the plants, then carefully dug and sorted the soil to remove the broken bits of their tuberous roots. Then I should have watched the area for emerging leaves and continued to dig up the roots. At some point a couple of applications of Roundup could have been used to finish off the stragglers.

In replanting the bed, I used plants with dark green foliage that simply disappeared into the gloom. Even the *Aquilegia* (columbine) I planted had dark blue blossoms that scarcely showed in the relatively deep shade. I also put in a few shade-loving bulbs, but I chose unwisely, planting *Galanthus nivalis* (common snowdrop) and *Scilla siberica* (Siberian squill). The tiny flowers are invisible from the house when they bloom in the chill of early spring.

My final error was in planting several other shade lovers willy-nilly without establishing big patches and clear areas of leaf contrast. No sense of unity emerged. To make matters worse, the columbine plants spread rapidly from seed, creating a jumble of foli-age around the scrappy hostas. The overall impression was dull, formless, and unattractive.

Sometimes It's Not Your Fault

Not all garden failures are the gardener's fault. You may be franti-cally studying to determine why a plant failed in your garden. Why is it unwell? What did you do to it? What should you have done? The truth is that even when you do all the right things, plants won't al-ways flourish. After a promising start and maybe even years of glo-rious bloom, a *Gypsophila paniculata* (baby's breath) may begin to dwindle. A few sad weeks later, in spite of all your careful ministra-tions, it is dead at your feet. *Gypsophila paniculata* is subject to crown rot. Plant two in the same garden and one may live five or six years while the other turns up its toes before its second season ends. Quit feeling guilty and go out and replace the ungrateful wretch.

To say that perennials live for many years is a generalization. Quite a few, generally called short-lived perennials, last only a few years. *Corydalis lutea,* syn. *Pseudofumaria lutea* and some varieties of *Aquilegia* (columbine) may live only two or three years. Fortu-nately, these are self-seeding and quick to reach mature size and begin blooming, so you may not realize that last year's plants are gone. Some short-lived perennials, though, are not self-sowers and are likely to leave unpleasant gaps when they move on to that great garden in the sky. *Campanula* (bellflower), *Dianthus deltoides* (maiden pinks), and *Aurinia saxatilis,* syn. *Alyssum saxatile* (basket of gold) will disappear from your garden, leaving no progeny be-hind to carry on their line. Perennials that may last from year to year in other locales seem to lose strength in the blazing heat of a Mid-western summer. Others are simply short-lived by nature. One way to avoid great gaps in the garden is to steer clear of perennials that won't last long and don't seed themselves freely. If you find you can't live without some of them, at least limit their number and plant them carefully to allow surrounding plants to fill the voids they will surely leave.

Some plants are so prone to certain diseases that prevention attempts are spit in the wind. If you grow *Monarda* (bee balm or bergamot) you will have powdery mildew at least some seasons and probably every season. You can try the newer, mildew-resistant cultivars to minimize the problem, but even they are likely to have mildew some of the time. Plant columbines and you can count on seeing leaf miners year after year. This is not your personal failure. This is the nature of the beast.

A number of perennials lavishly praised in garden books and catalogs may be suitable for other climates, but are difficult to grow in the heat of the Midwest: *Leucanthemum* x *superbum,* syn. *Chrysanthemum maximum* of gardens (Shasta daisy), *Gaillardia* 'Burgunder,' syn. 'Burgundy' (blanket flower), *Digitalis* (foxglove), delphiniums, many cultivars of *Heuchera* (coral flower or coral bells), *Veronica* (speedwell; the creeping sort, however, seem to thrive), and most *Primula* (primrose). These enchanting plants are disappointing in a hot climate, where they will sprawl, become diseased, bloom poorly, and live only two or three years at most. Even if they survive longer, they won't have the size, vigor, and healthful beauty they can attain elsewhere. Other plants will be disasters in the clay soil with which many of us are saddled. *Lavandula* (lavender) is highly touted in book after book without much said about the kind of soil it requires. Believe me, it is a disappointment when you plant it on even carefully amended clay soil.

8

Sequence of Bloom and Calendar of Garden Work

One of the most difficult parts of designing a garden is planning attractive groupings of plants that will bloom simultaneously. Plants are generally described vaguely as blooming in "early spring" or "midsummer," but even if you knew exactly when that was or how long it lasted the seasons referred to would probably be in some climate other than your own. To help you plan your Midwestern garden, I'm including this bloom sequence list geared to our part of the country. Obviously specific plants will not flower the same week throughout the Midwest, but they are likely to flower in the same *sequence*. Likewise, plants that bloom as companions in one part of the Midwest are likely to do so, too, in another.

Variations in geographical location, altitude, microclimate, rainfall, and seasonal mildness or severity all affect the timing of bloom, so no list can be definitive. A particular plant will not bloom at exactly the same time throughout our region or even in the same neighborhood. Weather varies year to year, affecting the flowers and how they bloom—both timing and length. This is especially true at the beginning and end of the growing season, when weather is most variable. Crocuses may bloom as early as late February or as late as the third week in March. Early heat combined with wind can stop daffodils in their tracks this year, while next year they may seem to go on forever in cool, cloudy weather. Midseason plants are more likely than others to bloom at about the same time year after year.

So that you can create groupings for effect, use this list to get an idea of which plants are likely to bloom in concert. Plan your garden for constant bloom throughout the growing season or plant for two-season bloom by selecting plants that flower at the appropriate times.

The list here can be a useful guide, but ideally you will begin to keep a sequence of bloom record for your own garden. Much has been written about keeping a garden diary and what to include, but it's a very personal matter. You may include sketches, plans, clippings, poetry, sappy descriptions of your favorite darlings, or arch satirical commentary. It doesn't really matter. The single thing that will make the diary useful to you in coming years is a record of when plants bloom and for how long. Once a week make the rounds of your garden, noting what plants are in bloom. This project will help you to learn not only bloom length and order but also plant names and how plants vary their bloom depending on the amount of sun or shade they get. If you don't want to go to the trouble of keeping a garden journal, just jot your own bloom times on the list here.

Sequence of Bloom

As you use the list for garden planning, remember that certain plants, due to their plant size, bloom size, length of bloom, and showiness, can be used as major design elements. Massed or repeated through a bed or garden, they can create unity at a particular season. Not all long-blooming plants fit this category, however. Some possess uninteresting foliage or flowers that are not particularly showy. Others bloom for a long period, but sporadically. Or a particular plant may be too small to make a splash. The boldface listings below indicate impact plants that might be considered chief features over four weeks or more around which you can build a garden design. In some cases (*Hosta,* for example) this long season of interest is provided by foliage rather than bloom. If several cultivars or species of one plant are named, it may take a mix of them to create several weeks of bloom.

Early Spring

Galanthus nivalis (common snowdrop): Late February to late March (three weeks)

Crocus vernus 'Pickwick' (Dutch crocus): Mid- to late March (two weeks)

Narcissus 'Tête-à-tête' (daffodil): Mid- to late March (one and a half weeks)

Chionodoxa luciliae, syn. *C. gigantea* (glory of the snow): Early to mid-April (two weeks)

Scilla siberica (Siberian squill): Early April to early May (five weeks)

Viola x *wittrockiana* (pansy), planted in bloom: Early April to late July (seventeen weeks)

Spring

Tulipa 'Heart's Delight' (tulip): Early to late April (two weeks)

Pulmonaria 'Roy Davidson' (lungwort): Early April to late May (eight weeks)

Mertensia pulmonarioides, syn. *M. virginica* (Virginia bluebells): Mid- to late April (two weeks)

Narcissus 'February Gold' (daffodil): Mid- to late April (one and a half weeks)

Narcissus 'Thalia' (daffodil): Mid-April to early May (four weeks)

Muscari (grape hyacinth): Mid-April to late May (five weeks)

Geum triflorum (prairie smoke): Mid-April to early June (seven weeks)

Viola tricolor (Johnny-jump-up): Mid-April to late August (nineteen weeks)

Pulmonaria saccharata 'Mrs. Moon' (lungwort): Late April to late May (four weeks)

Tulipa clusiana 'Cynthia' (tulip): Early May (two weeks)

Epimedium (barrenwort): Early to mid-May (one and a half weeks)

Tulipa 'Ballade' (lily-flowered tulip): Early to mid-May (three weeks)

Tulipa 'Mariette' (lily-flowered tulip): Early to mid-May (three weeks)

Tulipa 'West Point' (lily-flowered tulip): Early to mid-May (three weeks)

Iberis sempervirens (candytuft): Early to late May (three weeks)

Aquilegia canadensis 'Corbett' (Canada columbine): Early May to early June (seven weeks)

Brunnera macrophylla, syn. *Anchusa myosotidiflora* (Siberian bugloss): Early May to early June (four weeks)

Dicentra spectabilis (bleeding heart): Early May to early June (five weeks)

Corydalis lutea, syn. *Pseudofumaria lutea:* Early May to mid-June (six weeks)

Phlox divaricata (woodland phlox or wild sweet William): Early May to early June (five weeks)

Veronica 'Waterperry' (speedwell): Early May to early June (five weeks)

Dicentra spectabilis f. *alba* (white bleeding heart): Early May to early September, if deadheaded (seventeen weeks)

Convallaria (lily-of-the-valley): Mid- to late May (two weeks)

Galium odoratum, syn. *Asperula odorata* (sweet woodruff): Mid- to late May (three weeks)

***Aquilegia canadensis* (Canada columbine):** Mid-May to early June (four weeks)

Geranium 'Johnson's Blue': Mid-May to late June (seven weeks)

Tiarella wherryi, syn. *T. cordifolia* var. *collina* (Wherry's foamflower): Mid-May to late June (seven weeks)

Geranium phaeum (mourning widow): Mid-May to mid-July (nine weeks)

Calamintha grandiflora 'Variegata' (calamint): Mid-May to early September (sixteen weeks)

Baptisia australis (blue wild indigo, false indigo, or plains false indigo): Late May to early June (two weeks)

Iris pseudacorous (yellow flag): Late May to early June (two weeks)

Paeonia (peony): Late May to early June (two weeks)

Iris (tall bearded hybrids): Late May to mid-June (three weeks)

Leucanthemum vulgare, syn. *Chrysanthemum leucanthemum* (ox-eye daisy): Late May to late June (seven weeks)

***Heuchera* x *brizoides* 'Chatterbox' (coral flower or coral bells):** Late May to mid-July (seven weeks)

Early Summer

***Nepeta* x *faassenii*, syn. *N. mussinii* of gardens (catmint):** Late May to late August (fourteen weeks)

Geranium sanguineum var. *striatum*, syn. *G. sanguineum* var. *lancastriense*: Late May to mid-October (twenty-five weeks)

***Iris* 'Ego' (Siberian iris):** Early June (1 week)

***Rosa glauca*, syn. *R. rubrifolia* (rose):** Flowers, early to mid-June (1 week); hips, July through September (12 weeks)

Digitalis purpurea 'Excelsior' (common foxglove): Early to late June (three weeks)

Iris **'Caesar's Brother' (Siberian iris):** Early to late June (three weeks)

Iris **'White Swirl' (Siberian iris):** Early to late June (three weeks)

Rosa **'Mary Rose' (rose):** Heavy first bloom, early to late June (three weeks); light second bloom, mid-July to late October (thirteen weeks)

Alchemilla mollis **(lady's mantle):** Early June to mid-July (five weeks)

Allium schoenoprasum (chives): Early June to mid-July (six weeks)

Clematis lanuginosa 'Candida': Early June to mid-July (four weeks)

Salvia officinalis (common sage): Early June to mid-July (six weeks)

Lychnis coronaria **(rose campion):** Early June to mid-August (ten weeks)

Achillea **'Moonshine' (yarrow):** Early June to early September (twelve weeks)

Digitalis x *mertonensis:* Early June to early September (twelve weeks)

Rosa **'Bonica' (rose):** Early June to late October (nineteen weeks)

Delphinium: Mid-June to mid-July (five weeks)

Midsummer

Clematis 'Nelly Moser': June (3 weeks)

Clematis viticella: Mid-June to early July (three weeks)

Astilbe **'Brautschleier,' syn.** *A.* **'Bridal Veil' (false spirea):** Late June to mid-July (two weeks)

Gypsophila paniculata 'Bristol Fairy' (baby's breath): First bloom, late June to mid-July (two weeks); second bloom, late July to late August (four weeks)

Consolida (larkspur): Late June to late July (four weeks)

Lilium 'Bonnie' (Asiatic hybrid lily): Late June to mid-July (two weeks)

Hosta sieboldiana var. *elegans* (hosta or plantain lily): Late June to late July (three weeks)

Filipendula purpurea (Japanese meadowsweet): Late June to early August (one and a half weeks)

Lilium regale (regal lily): Late June to early August (one and a half weeks)

***Nepeta* 'Six Hills Giant' (catmint):** Late June to mid-August (seven weeks)

Coreopsis verticillata 'Moonbeam' (threadleaf tickseed): Late June to late September (fourteen weeks)

***Rudbeckia fulgida* var. *sullivantii* 'Goldsturm':** Late June to late September (thirteen weeks)

Zinnia: Late June to late September (thirteen weeks)

Antirrhinum Liberty Series (snapdragon): Late June to frost (fifteen to eighteen weeks)

Nicotiana alata, syn. *N. affinis* (flowering tobacco): Late June to frost (fifteen to eighteen weeks)

Petunia: Late June to frost (fifteen to eighteen weeks)

Tagetes (marigold): Late June to frost (fifteen to eighteen weeks)

Borago officinalis (borage): Early July to late September (twelve weeks)

Lobularia maritima, syn. *Alyssum maritimum* (sweet alyssum): Early July to late October (sixteen weeks)

***Astilbe* 'Sprite' (false spirea):** Mid- to late July (two weeks)

Hemerocallis (daylily) 'Little Grapette': Mid- to late July (two weeks)

Anethum graveolens (dill): Mid-July to early August (three weeks)

Astilbe chinensis var. *taquetii* 'Superba' (false spirea): Mid-July to early August (two weeks)

Hemerocallis (daylily) 'Daydream Believer': Mid-July to early August (3 weeks)

Astilbe chinensis var. *pumila* (false spirea): Mid-July to mid-August (four weeks)

Digitalis lutea (straw foxglove): Mid-July to mid-August (four weeks)

Hemerocallis (daylily) 'Bowl of Roses': Mid-July to mid-August (four weeks)

Hemerocallis (daylily) 'Little Fat Dazzler': Mid-July to mid-August (3 weeks)

Hemerocallis (daylily) 'Prairie Blue Eyes': Mid-July to mid-August (4 weeks)

Echinops ritro (small globe thistle): Mid-July to late August (five weeks)

Phlox paniculata (garden phlox): Mid-July to late August (six weeks)

Platycodon grandiflorus (balloon flower): Mid-July to early September (six weeks)

Thalictrum rochebrunianum: 'Lavender Mist' (meadow rue): Mid-July to late September (ten weeks)

Aster x *frikartii* 'Mönch': Mid-July to frost (thirteen weeks)

Salvia farinacea 'Victoria' (mealycup sage): Mid-July to frost (thirteen to sixteen weeks)

Tanacetum parthenium, syn. *Chrysanthemum parthenium* (feverfew): Mid-July to frost (thirteen to sixteen weeks)

Lilium 'Casa Blanca' (Oriental hybrid lily): Late July to mid-August (two weeks)

Lilium 'Pink Virtuoso' (Oriental hybrid lily): Late July to mid-August (two weeks)

Late Summer

Perovskia atriplicifolia (**Russian sage**): Early August to late September (eight weeks)

Thymophylla tenuiloba, syn. *Dyssodia tenuiloba* (Dahlberg daisy or golden fleece): Early August to late September (eight weeks)

Buddleia davidii 'Lochinch' (**butterfly bush**): Early August to late October (twelve weeks)

Calamintha nepeta (**lesser calamint**): Early August to late October (twelve weeks)

Cleome (**spider flower**): Early August to late October (twelve weeks)

Fall

Clematis terniflora, syn. *C. maximowicziana* or *C. paniculata* (sweet autumn clematis): Early to mid-September (one and a half weeks)

Boltonia asteroides: September (four weeks)

Anemone tomentosa 'Robustissima,' syn. *A. vitifolia* 'Robustissima' (**grape-leaf anemone**): Early September to frost (six to nine weeks)

Aster novae-angliae 'Andenken an Alma Pötschke,' syn. 'Alma Pötschke' (**New England aster**): Early September to late October (seven weeks)

Chrysanthemum: Early September to frost (six to nine weeks)

Origanum (oregano): September (four weeks)

Calendar of Garden Work

The following brief outline doesn't cover every last thing you need to do in your garden. This schedule covers only projects that need to be accomplished at specific times, since most garden work can be done as you have time for it. Check to determine the average spring frost-free date and the average fall first frost date in your area.

Spring Projects

Eight weeks before the frost-free date

- ⮌ Begin raking leaves off flower beds, finishing in about two weeks.

Six weeks before the frost-free date

- ⮌ Edge flower beds.
- ⮌ Prune roses.
- ⮌ Prune shrubs that bloom on new wood. Shrubs that bloom on old wood, such as forsythia and *Syringa* (lilac), should not be pruned until after they bloom.
- ⮌ Cut back *Buddleia davidii* (butterfly bush) and *Perovskia atriplicifolia* (Russian sage) to about twelve inches from the ground.
- ⮌ Cut back herbaceous plants that were not cut back in autumn.
- ⮌ Begin perennial planting, including transplanting perennials that bloom in summer or fall.

Four weeks before the frost-free date

- ⮌ Plant *Viola* x *wittrockiana* (pansy).
- ⮌ Prune clematis vines that bloom on new wood.

Two weeks before the frost-free date:

- ✎ Finish planting and transplanting perennials.
- ✎ Plant *Antirrhinum* (snapdragon) and *Lobularia maritima,* syn. *Alyssum maritimum* (sweet alyssum).

Frost-free date:

- ✎ Plant annuals, finishing within two weeks.

Fall Projects

Six weeks before the first frost:

- ✎ Plant perennials and transplant perennials that bloom in spring or summer.

First frost:

- ✎ Cut down and compost healthy foliage of annuals, biennials, and perennials, excluding those that must be pruned back in spring and those that remain green throughout winter.
- ✎ Cut down and dispose of unhealthy foliage.

9

Building a Garden Library

There are three ways to learn about gardening: get some dirt under your fingernails, ask questions of gardeners and experts, and read. Reading is the fastest way to gain a solid base of knowledge. It's also lots of fun. A good garden reference library can go a long way toward filling the gaps and correcting the gaffs of flower catalogs, too. Here are a few suggestions.

Encyclopedias

Brickell, Christopher, ed. *American Horticultural Society Encyclopedia of Garden Plants.* New York: Macmillan, 1989.

This is simply the finest reference around for the passionate gardener. Arranged by scientific name, it also provides an index by common name. The text section at the back provides descriptions of plants and their varieties and refers you to the photographic section for pictures of specific varieties and still more information. The photographic section is arranged by type of plant: Trees, conifers, shrubs, roses, climbers, grasses, ferns, perennials, annuals and biennials, rock plants, bulbs, water plants, and cacti and other succulents. Each type of plant is subdivided. Perennials, for instance, are separated into large, medium, and small, with big subsections on important perennials like chrysanthemums and hostas. These subsections are arranged by color. This way of organizing the pictures makes the book outstanding for design purposes. Inclusion of trees, shrubs, grasses, and so on makes it an invaluable landscaping resource.

Coverage is very thorough: hardiness zone, sun/shade requirements, moisture needs, height and width at maturity, and care information. This is an expensive book, but the cost of color reproduction pushes many garden books to thirty dollars or more. This one, at about twice that figure, is worth half a dozen of the thirty-dollar kind. Buy it. You'll never regret it.

Brickell, Christopher, and Judith D. Zuk, eds. *The American Horticultural Society A-Z Encyclopedia of Garden Plants.* New York: DK Publishing, 1997.

Another great tome from the American Horticultural Society and Christopher Brickell is this more recent volume, very similar in content and coverage, but differently arranged. Brickell and Zuk give a few pages at the beginning to some basics like propagation and pruning, but the vast majority of the book is a straight alphabetical encyclopedia of plants. The arrangement is not useful for design purposes since plants are not grouped by type, size, and color. However, it does cover new plant introductions. Further, all the photos and information on a particular plant appear in one listing. Ideally your garden library would contain both volumes, but if only one fits your budget, this more recent work may be easier to find at a bookstore.

Armitage, Allan M. *Herbaceous Perennial Plants.* Athens, Ga.: Varsity Press, 1989.

Although Armitage includes a handful of color photographs bound together in the center of this work and a scattering of black-and-white illustrations, the real point here is his information-packed text. This is an encyclopedia of important garden perennial plants and their varieties and cultivars. Armitage covers only herbaceous (nonwoody) and bulbous perennial plants. Descriptions include plant height and width, hardiness zone, bloom season, useful care information, and much more. Although this is a sound scholarly work, descriptions are easy to understand and the style is an informal pleasure to read. Armitage frequently offers helpful advice about differing performance of plants in the North and South. This can be a trifle confusing for those of us living in the center of the country, but generally you can assume that plants that suffer from heat and humidity in the South are likely to have some degree of the same problem in the hot Midwest.

Armitage, Allan M. *Armitage's Garden Perennials: A Color Encyclopedia.* Portland, Ore.: Timber Press, 2000.

If a textbook daunts you, try Armitage's popularized work instead. He features what he considers the most interesting, important, or overlooked plants, offers brief and personal comments, and illustrates the book with almost 1,500 color photographs in a handy alphabetical listing.

Cox, Jeffrey. *Perennial All-Stars.* Emmaus, Penn.: Rodale Press, 1998.

This compendium of the author's choice of the 150 best perennial plants gives a generous amount of information in a double-page spread for each plant. This is a first-rate reference for beginners because it offers identifying color photographs, descriptions, care information, propagation techniques, and suggestions for companion planting. The author is an Easterner who gardens in northern California.

Trees and Shrubs

Dirr, Michael A. *Manual of Woody Landscape Plants: Their Identification, Ornamental Characteristics, Culture, Propagation, and Uses.* 4th ed. Champaign, Ill.: Stipes, 1990.

The longer you garden, the more you value shrubs and trees and the more questions you have about them. This book answers all those questions. Known simply as "Dirr" among horticultural professionals, this magnificent tome is a wonderful blend of scientific detail and personal commentary. I especially appreciate the author's comments about how plants fare in different parts of the country. He also gives generous information about mature size. Dirr is invaluable in choosing shrubs and trees. You've decided to plant a *Viburnum* in that shady spot? Check Dirr to decide which one would be best. This is a textbook, so look for it in a university bookstore.

Dirr, Michael A. *Dirr's Hardy Trees and Shrubs: An Illustrated Encyclopedia.* Portland, Ore.: Timber Press, 1997.

This marvelous volume on trees and shrubs from the expert is heavily illustrated with color photographs. Over five hundred species are covered in text and photographs. Though the book lacks the in-depth coverage and detail on propagation and care provided in his other book, the photos in this one make it a valuable tool for selecting trees for the landscape. The text is more accessible for the home gardener, and the book is likely to be easier to find in a bookstore or library, too.

Design

Harper, Pamela J. *Designing with Perennials*. New York: Macmillan, 1991.

This is the best book out there on how to design a garden. Everything you need to know is in this one volume. The sooner in your gardening life you read and absorb it the better because its principles should be applied to your garden as soon as possible. It isn't an easy read for a beginner. Harper refers to many plants you may not have heard of. Keep your *American Horticultural Society Encyclopedia of Garden Plants* handy. Reread the book five years later to soak up its wisdom all over again. By then you'll be familiar with many more plants and the book will be far easier to comprehend.

Harper is English by birth and American by residence. She has had a long career in gardening, half of it in England, half in the United States, where she has gardened in widely different climates. This background gives her a rare perspective. Her range of knowledge is impressive and her artistic flare enviable. The excellent color photos in this book are by the author and clearly illustrate specific points.

Harper, Pamela. *Color Echoes: Harmonizing Color in the Garden*. New York: Macmillan, 1994.

Here Harper expands upon her treatment of color, teaching you to see plant combinations differently and to appreciate the value of color *repetition*, while every other design book seems to speak of color largely in terms of *contrast*.

Cottage and Romantic Gardening

Hensel, Margaret. *English Cottage Gardening for American Gardeners.* New York: W. W. Norton, 1992.

If you yearn for a cottage garden or relish the romantic in garden design, you will love this book. Both text and photographs are full of ideas that help bring into focus exactly what elements combine to create the cozy charm of a cottage garden.

Wilder, Louise Beebe. *Color in My Garden: An American Gardener's Palette.* New York: Atlantic Monthly Press, 1990.

This reprint of a book originally published in 1919 is surprisingly fresh and readable. The author's enjoyable and informal style somehow conveys a solid grasp of what it takes to accomplish the immensely complicated task of creating a lavish, romantic flower garden.

Grooming

DiSabato-Aust, Tracy. *The Well-Tended Perennial Garden: Planting and Pruning Techniques.* Portland, Ore.: Timber Press, 1998.

A practical and unique guide, this book is packed with specific information about how and when to pinch, prune, deadhead, stake, and otherwise groom the garden to achieve maximum bloom and beauty. The author, who lives and gardens in Ohio, amply answers questions about how to care for plants once they're in the ground.

Index

Index

Index

Index

Mourning widow (*Geranium phaeum*), 83,
175
Mulch, 41, 145–46
    compost as, 146
    grass clippings as, 146
    winter, 146
Muscari (grape hyacinth), 71–72, 174
Myrtle (*Vinca minor,* dwarf periwinkle), 72

Narcissus (daffodil), 66–69
    'Carlton,' 68
    'February Gold,' 68, 173
    foliage of, 64
    in garden design, 64, 69
    'Tête-à-Tête,' 68, 173
    'Thalia,' 68, 174
    transplanting, 68
Naturalization, 148
Nepeta (catmint), 87–89
    cataria (catnip), 88–89
    cutting back, 89
    x *faassenii,* syn. *N. mussinii* of gardens,
        19, 87–88, 177
    shearing, 147
    'Six Hills Giant,' 88, 177
Nicotiana (tobacco plant), 117–19
    affinis, syn. *N. alata* (flowering tobacco),
        117–18, 177
    langsdorfii, 118–19
    'Lime Green,' 118
    sylvestris, 118
Nigella damascena (love-in-a-mist), 9–10

Ocimum basilicum (basil), 50, 128
Origanum (oregano), 179
Ox-eye daisy (*Leucanthemum vulgare,* syn.
    Chrysanthemum leucanthemum), 30, 175

Paeonia (peony), 175
Painted fern, Japanese (*Athyrium niponicum,*
    syn. *A. goeringianum*), 93
Pansy (*Viola* x *wittrockiana*), 55–56, 73–74, 173
Papaver (poppy), 9–10
Parthenocissus tricuspidata (Boston ivy), 17
Pea staking, 152
Pelargonium (geranium), 83
Peony (*Paeonia*), 175
Periwinkle, dwarf (*Vinca minor,* myrtle), 72

Perovskia atriplicifolia (Russian sage), 128–29
    bloom time of, 179
    'Filagran,' 129
    'Longin,' 129
Pests
    aphids, 158–60
    leaf miner, 81
    rabbits, 160
    slugs, 156–58
    snails, 156
    squirrels, 160–61
    tarnished plant bug, 125
Petunia, 116, 177
Phlox divaricata (woodland phlox, wild
    sweet William), 77–78, 174
Phlox paniculata (garden phlox), 62, 178
Pinching, 146–47
Plains false indigo (*Baptisia australis,* blue
    wild indigo, false indigo), 59, 85–86
    bloom time of, 175
    spacing of, 54
Plantain lily (*Hosta*), 105–7
    as companion to *Astilbe* (false spirea), 107
    in heat wave, 3
    H. 'Krossa Regal,' 93, 107
    H. sieboldiana
        'Frances Williams,' 107
        var. *elegans,* 59, 106–7, 177
    repetition of, 19
    spacing of, 54
Plant hardiness zones, USDA, 3–4
Planting and transplanting, 50, 57–58
    marking plants for future, 57
    size of hole, 56
    spacing plants, 54–55
    to increase stock, 58
Planting time, 55, 57, 180, 181
    annuals, 55, 181
    Antirrhinum (snapdragon), 55–56, 181
    Lobularia maritima, syn. *Alyssum mariti-*
        mum (sweet alyssum), 55–56, 181
    perennials, 55, 180, 181
    Viola x *wittrockiana* (pansy), 55–56, 180
Plant names, 15–16
Platycodon grandiflorus (balloon flower), 62,
    178
Polygonatum odoratum 'Variegatum' (fra-
    grant Solomon's seal), 59

Index

197

LINDA HILLEGASS was raised in a family of diehard gardeners and has been gardening in the hot Midwest for more than twenty years. A former librarian, she now works full-time in the three bookstores she owns with her husband. Gardening is her passion. Her gardening publications include a chapter in *Perennials: Toward Continuous Bloom*, edited by Ann Lovejoy.

Typeset in 11.5/15 Minion
with Palette display
Designed by Dennis Roberts
Composed by Jim Proefrock
at the University of Illinois Press
Manufactured by Friesens Corporation

University of Illinois Press
1325 South Oak Street
Champaign, IL 61820-6903
www.press.uillinois.edu